Architecture and Its Sculpture in Viceregal Mexico

D1136331

Architecture and Its Sculpture in Viceregal Mexico

ROBERT J. MULLEN

UNIVERSITY OF TEXAS PRESS, AUSTIN

To Anne

Copyright © 1997 by the University of Texas Press
All rights reserved
Printed in the United States of America

First edition, 1997

All reproduction rights to the photographs by Robert J. Mullen
are held by the Benson Latin American Collection,
University of Texas at Austin, Austin TX 78712. The photographs
may not be reproduced without prior permission from the
Benson Latin American Collection.

Requests for permission to reproduce the text from this work
should be sent to Permissions,
University of Texas Press, Box 7819, Austin TX 78713-7819.

∞The paper used in this publication meets the minimum
requirements of American National Standard for Information
Sciences—Permanence of Paper for Printed Library Materials,
ANSI Z39.48-1984.

LIBRARY OF CONGRESS
CATALOGING-IN-PUBLICATION DATA
Mullen, Robert James.
Architecture and its sculpture in viceregal Mexico /
by Robert J. Mullen.
— 1st ed.
p.   cm.
Includes bibliographical references and index.
ISBN 0-292-75209-1. — ISBN 0-292-75210-5 (pbk.)
1. Architecture, colonial—Mexico.   2. Architecture—Mexico.
3. Decoration and ornament, Architectural—Mexico.   I. Title.
NA753.M85   1997
720′.972—dc21   96-51256

Contents

Preface, Conventions, Acknowledgments

＊— ☰◆☰ —＊

PURPOSE

A number of authors have addressed the architecture and sculpture of colonial Mexico. There is George Kubler and Martin Soria, *Art and Architecture in Spain and Portugal and Their American Dominions;* George Kubler, *Mexican Architecture of the Sixteenth Century;* John McAndrew, *The Open-Air Churches of Sixteenth-Century Mexico;* Robert Mullen, *Dominican Architecture in Sixteenth-Century Oaxaca;* Manuel Toussaint, *Colonial Art in Mexico.* Monographs and regional studies also exist. None, however, serve the needs of the general reader or college student who seeks a comprehensive account of architecture and its attendant sculpture for the entire colonial period. It is my intention to satisfy that need with this book.

ORGANIZATION

I estimate nearly 100,000 churches and civic buildings were constructed in Mexico between 1530 and 1800, the period of its colonial architecture. I see colonial Mexico as enveloped in two worlds, that of the city and that of the pueblo. Many structures are quite ordinary. Others reflect the pageantry of imperial urban display, works of accomplished architects. A surprising number of churches are distinctive, even unique. In this work I shall concentrate in chapters 2 through 6 on those features distinguishing the architecture and sculpture of each world, organized into three time frames—the formative era, from the 1540s into the 1600s; a transitional phase, from 1650 to 1750; and the age of fulfillment, from 1750 to 1800. Chapter 7 is devoted to the seventeenth- and eighteenth-century mission churches in Spain's northern frontier, our Southwest.

ACKNOWLEDGMENTS

Most photographs and drawings are mine. The task of making the prints, however, was almost entirely accomplished by David Zook. He created hundreds, each made to maximize half-tone reproduction, each a work of art. He met the challenge of transforming color slides into black and white negatives and, eventually, prints. Some illustrations, of varying sizes and quality, were found in books. These he photographed with consummate skill, their prints matching others perfectly. I am truly indebted to David Zook for the professional capability and personal care he put into the task. When ill health made difficult the final task of having the negatives made into quality prints, David took on the role of film manager. In doing so he relieved me of a great burden. His performance was outstanding. Thanks, Dave.

I owe a debt of gratitude to Lic. Cecilia Gutiérrez Arriola, Director of the Photographic Archives of the Instituto de Investigaciones Estéticas, Universidad Nacional Autónoma de México, for providing a number of excellent photographs either of places I lacked or of higher quality. Also in Mexico I wish to thank Arq. Víctor Jiménez Muñoz, director of the publishing firm CODEX Editores, for his strong support. He performed the daunting task of checking the manuscript for accuracy and clarity; his suggestions were meticulously followed.

Among my colleagues I am indebted to Dr. Bernard L. Fontana and Dr. Norman Neuerburg. They were unstinting in their assistance concerning, respectively, the missions of Arizona and California. Another colleague, Mardith Shuetz-Miller, associated with the Arizona State Museum, played a key role in the final review, providing insights and offering many solid suggestions. In San Antonio, Dr. Rosalind Z. Rock, Park Historian, was instrumental in obtaining measured drawings of the San Antonio missions and other valuable data. I am indebted to Mónica Guajardo M. for creating the excellent pen and ink drawing that is now Fig. 3.1.

I doubt the manuscript would have been accepted without the critical and corrective eye of my editor, Dr. Janet F. Williams McDonald, a very busy medical person. I can never sufficiently express my appreciation nor conceal my wonder.

My patient and ever-understanding wife, Anne, provided constant encouragement and "protection" from romping grandchildren. To her, with all my love, I dedicate this book.

WORDS AND MEASUREMENTS

A number of Spanish words have no proper English equivalent. After their first italicized appearance they are used as normal English words. For example *convento* becomes convento. Meaning is made evident contextually. A glossary has been added for convenience. I have chosen not to hyphenate such words as "prehispanic" or "neoclassic."

"Mexico" can mean either the capital city or the nation. Where the context is not absolutely clear, the word will be identified as one or the other. Up to 1820 the term "The Viceregency of New Spain" (Nueva España) was used to identify today's Mexico (which at one time included areas in the United States from the Atlantic to the Pacific oceans.) As a nation, Mexico now has 31 states plus the Federal District (essentially Mexico City). In the text states are shown in parentheses following the place name, e.g., Tlaxcala (Tlaxcala).

Measurements are metric. One meter equals 39.31 inches.

MAP ADVISORY

Many of the pueblos mentioned in the book are difficult to locate. The maps in this book were enlarged in order to more readily show the pueblos' relative location. For this purpose Mexico was divided into three zones—north, central, and south. In each of these zones only the states and places pertinent to the book are named, except that some key places have been added to assist in orientation. With a good road map of Mexico, such as that available through the American Automobile Association, the actual location of the pueblo or city can be pinpointed, and the roads and routes thereto can be determined. The scale of the normal road map for all of Mexico is not large enough to show all the places mentioned in Oaxaca. To locate those pueblos it will be necessary to purchase a road map of that state. Some of the cited places can be reached only by high-wheeled vehicle.

The States of Mexico

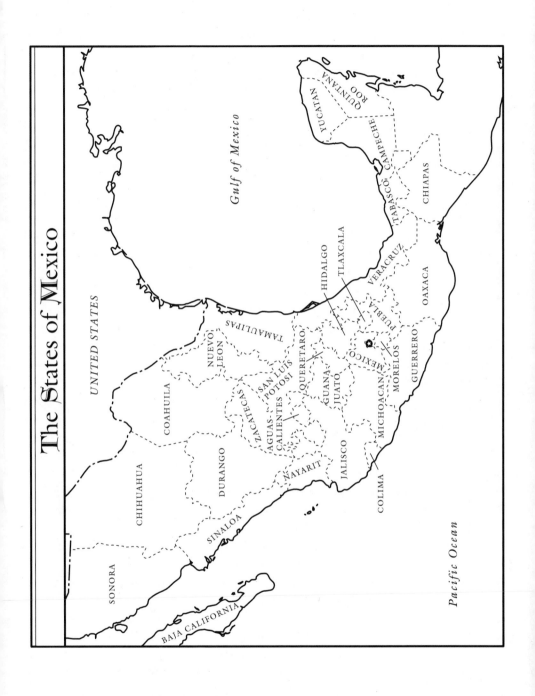

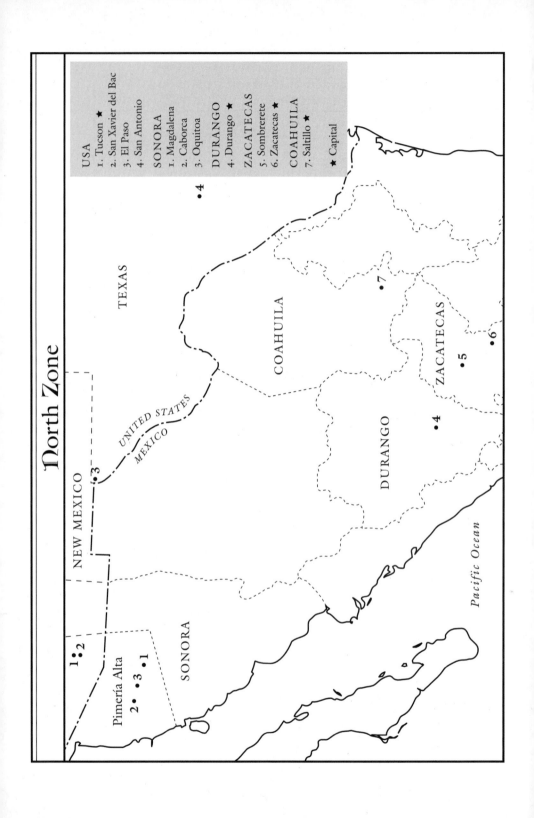

North Zone

USA
1. Tucson ★
2. San Xavier del Bac
3. El Paso
4. San Antonio
SONORA
1. Magdalena
2. Caborca
3. Oquitoa
DURANGO
4. Durango ★
ZACATECAS
5. Sombrerete
6. Zacatecas ★
COAHUILA
7. Saltillo ★
    ★ Capital

NEW MEXICO

TEXAS

Pimería Alta

SONORA

UNITED STATES
MEXICO

COAHUILA

DURANGO

ZACATECAS

Pacific Ocean

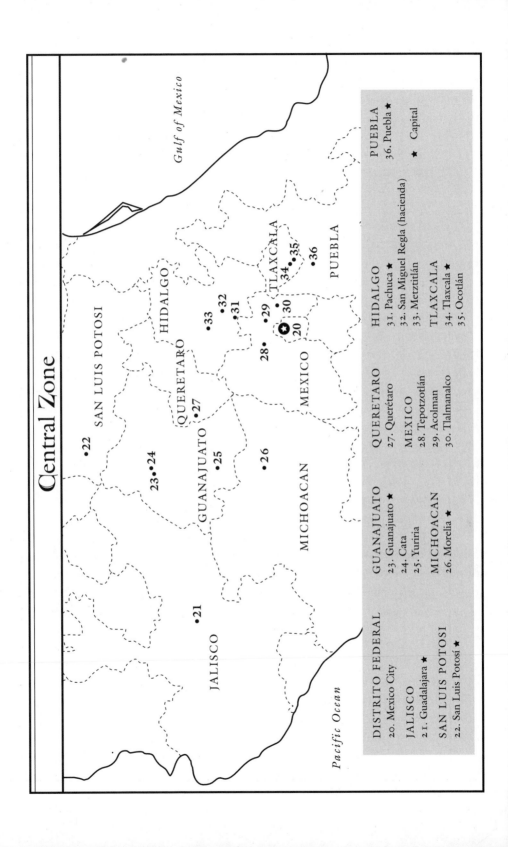

Central Zone

Gulf of Mexico

Pacific Ocean

SAN LUIS POTOSI

HIDALGO

QUERETARO

GUANAJUATO

MICHOACAN

JALISCO

MEXICO

TLAXCALA

PUEBLA

DISTRITO FEDERAL
20. Mexico City

JALISCO
21. Guadalajara ★

SAN LUIS POTOSI
22. San Luis Potosí ★

GUANAJUATO
23. Guanajuato ★
24. Cata
25. Yuriria

MICHOACAN
26. Morelia ★

QUERETARO
27. Querétaro

MEXICO
28. Tepotzotlán
29. Acolman
30. Tlalmanalco

HIDALGO
31. Pachuca ★
32. San Miguel Regla (hacienda)
33. Metztitlán

TLAXCALA
34. Tlaxcala ★
35. Ocotlán

PUEBLA
36. Puebla ★

★ Capital

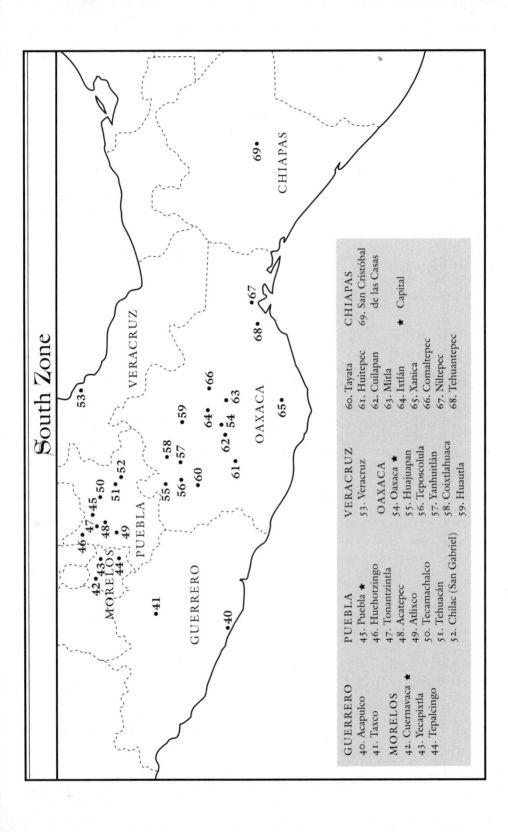

South Zone

GUERRERO
40. Acapulco
41. Taxco

MORELOS
42. Cuernavaca ★
43. Yecapixtla
44. Tepalcingo

PUEBLA
45. Puebla ★
46. Huehotzingo
47. Tonantzintla
48. Acatepec
49. Atlixco
50. Tecamachalco
51. Tehuacán
52. Chilac (San Gabriel)

VERACRUZ
53. Veracruz

OAXACA
54. Oaxaca ★
55. Huajuapan
56. Teposcolula
57. Yanhuitlán
58. Coixtlahuaca
59. Huautla

60. Tayata
61. Huitepec
62. Cuilapan
63. Mitla
64. Ixtlán
65. Xanica
66. Comaltepec
67. Niltepec
68. Tehuantepec

CHIAPAS
69. San Cristóbal
    de las Casas

★ Capital

Frontier

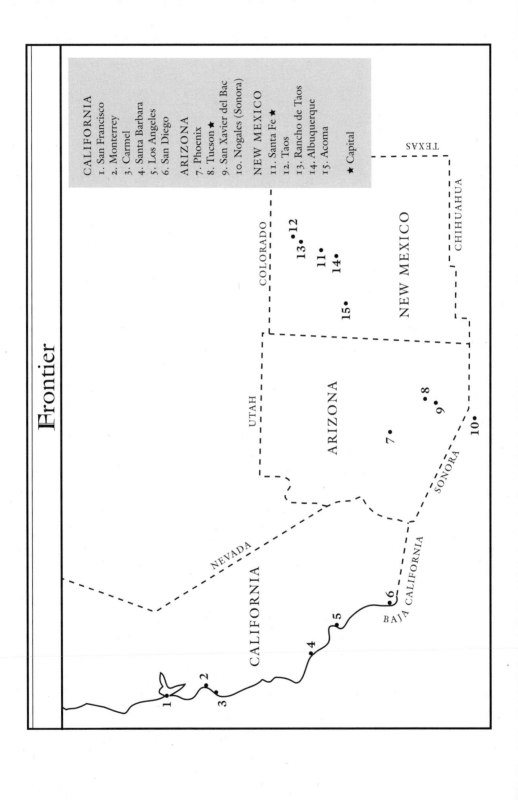

CALIFORNIA
1. San Francisco
2. Monterrey
3. Carmel
4. Santa Barbara
5. Los Angeles
6. San Diego

ARIZONA
7. Phoenix
8. Tucson ★
9. San Xavier del Bac
10. Nogales (Sonora)

NEW MEXICO
11. Santa Fe ★
12. Taos
13. Rancho de Taos
14. Albuquerque
15. Acoma

★ Capital

1

Overview

‣‒ ⩴♦⩴ ‒‣

IN Mesoamerica—the region from central Mexico to Guatemala—at least a dozen cultural entities arose, peaked and faded away over a period of 2,500 years before the arrival of Europeans. Each culture is readily identifiable through characteristic architecture and relief sculpture. This architecture generally consisted of compact structures, at times quite tall, massed around an open ceremonial court. Large interior spaces were not constructed, and the vault was unknown. The dynamic forces that engendered these distinctive cultures and their ceremonial centers had, by 1000 AD, largely run their course. Abandoned, these great sites reverted to nature to await their discovery centuries later. In 1519, when the Spaniards came ashore, only a few ceremonial centers were active. One of these was Tenochtitlán, the seat of power of the Aztecs, who controlled most of central Mexico until they were overpowered by the Spanish. Today the excavated ruins of Tenochtitlán's great ceremonial court lie in the heart of Mexico City.

Spurred by the immense profits gained from trade with Asia, the result of Portugal's discovery of an all-water route, Europe was gripped with "colonization fever." After the discovery of the Americas, every European nation with the means and the money sought to acquire foreign lands. Power and wealth were the driving forces. Spain and Portugal, however, had an additional objective—to convert and to acculturate. Conversion would transform new subjects into Christians and acculturation would, in due course, produce citizens for Spain and Portugal. In the early 1520s, Spain's monarchs, King Ferdinand and Queen Isabella, sent friars as missionaries to the area that is now Mexico to help realize that objective. Soon thereafter the Viceregency of Nueva España was established.

In just over 25 years a small group of friars, filled with an apostolic zeal, converted the population of central Mexico and much of that of the Yucatán. By the 1550s, itinerant missionaries had become settled pastors with parish churches in long-established "Indian" communities they called *pueblos*. Now the need arose for an architecture unknown to Mesoamerica—large volumes enclosed with vaults.

The rapid conversion of millions gave rise to unprecedented demand for churches. Relatively sudden and overwhelming spiritual needs were met with open-air churches. The "temporary" sanctuary was covered, but the populace attended Mass in an outdoor area designated for worship. Although meant to be used only until a "proper" church could be constructed, many stone sanctuaries have survived. They constitute Mexico's unique contribution to the history of architecture. By constructing these open-air churches the friars unwittingly assisted in the successful transition to the Catholic faith of peoples long accustomed to religious ceremonies in the open.

Only a few pastors had any formal training in architecture or sculpture. Fortunately, they settled among skilled native artisans and masons. Ideas and technical processes common to Europe were transmitted to indigenous peoples whose language lacked the vocabulary for such ideas and techniques. In this halting, often confusing process, began that fusion of cultures that produced "Mexican" art and architecture. As a result sixteenth-century pueblo churches are a unique blend of European and Mesoamerican values, traditions, and techniques.

Many pueblo churches are adorned with distinctive sculpture. Mesoamerican images were cut in a flat, two-dimensional relief, like dough shaped by a cookie cutter. Symbolism, not realism, was the objective. This was the heritage of the indigenous sixteenth-century sculptor totally unfamiliar with Renaissance ideals of three-dimensional realism. The vocabulary of the Renaissance was used, but seldom was its syntax mastered. In this blending of traditions a new form of relief sculpture was created, one so distinctive and powerful it has a special name—*tequitqui*.

Thus began the "Columbian exchange," the transfer of plants, animals, peoples, cultures and diseases from one continent to another. The introduction of chicken pox, measles, smallpox and influenza into the New World had devastating results. Epidemics caused great loss of life among the native peoples. Expansion slowed drastically in the seventeenth century. Missionary zeal was replaced by power struggles between the religious orders and the bishops, who won. New construction was no longer concentrated in the pueblos but focused instead on bishoprics and their city cathedrals. Only toward the end of that century had economic and social conditions improved to a level that could again foster growth and expansion.

The eighteenth century in New Spain witnessed a remarkable transformation. Wealth, public and private, accumulated rapidly. Churches, convents, colleges, town houses and other civic structures blossomed. This was the era of the "silver" churches of north-central Mexico. Styles became fanciful and florid, surface decoration profuse. Densely sculptured altarpieces sheathed in gold, and wall surfaces covered with gold-trimmed white stucco dazzled the eye. After 1750, altarpieces with slender, tapering squared columns (*estípites*) became the reigning style. In the facade estípites of stone replicated the intricate carvings of wood altarpieces. Brilliant but evanescent, this "Churrigueresque" style lasted scarcely fifty years.

In the seventeenth and eighteenth centuries missionary efforts were concentrated on Nueva España's northern rim, extending from the Gulf of Mexico to the Pacific. By the mid-seventeenth century, Franciscan missionaries had founded twenty-four missions in New Mexico. Meanwhile, Jesuit missionaries were active in northern Sonora, not becoming active in southern Arizona until the eighteenth century. In that same century it was the Franciscans who evangelized the natives of Texas and California.

The end of the colonial period, artistically and architecturally, was signaled even before 1800 by the return to the strict canons of neoclassicism. Politically, the Viceregency ended in 1821 when Mexico achieved independence.

2

Urban Beginnings

The Cities

In Mesoamerica, the ceremonial center with its many pyramidal structures combined the practical matters of government with the ceremonial functions of religion. Consequently, there was no distinction between civil and religious architecture in prehispanic times. Soon after
the Conquest, however, the need for both civil and religious architecture became imperative as new cities were founded and native communities were urbanized. The plaza became the core feature in both.
Administrative centers, schools, hospitals, water supplies, defenses
and, above all, churches were needed where none had ever existed.

The term "city" will be used here to refer to Spanish settlements,
"pueblo" to indigenous communities. Foremost among the cities of
Nueva España was Mexico City, founded in 1521 on the site of the
former Aztec capitol, Tenochtitlán. Within a few years "strategic"
cities were founded throughout the country: Tlaxcala (in the State of
Tlaxcala), Puebla (Puebla), Morelia (Michoacán), Guanajuato (Guanajuato), Guadalajara (Jalisco), Querétaro (Querétaro), Oaxaca (Oaxaca), Mérida (Yucatán) and San Cristóbal de las Casas (Chiapas).
Other cities, such as Zacatecas (Zacatecas), San Luis Potosí (San Luis
Potosí) and Durango (Durango) were also founded in the sixteenth
century, once valuable minerals were discovered there. Major ports
were established as well during this century. Veracruz (Veracruz), as
old as Mexico City, became the gateway to Mexico.

Spaniards were enjoined not to go to the Indian pueblos, and the Indians were discouraged from entering a city until it was completed. The latter restriction was diligently ignored, for who else could build the cities but the Indians? Their numbers in Mexico City were sufficient to cause the Franciscans there to construct, very early on, a *capilla de indios*. This open-air chapel, named San José de los Naturales, had an interior so large it accommodated the catafalque for the funeral services for Charles V. Urban designs were soon regulated and, in 1573, the Spanish sovereign, Philip II, promulgated the City Planning Ordinances of the Laws of the Indies.[1]

The main plaza is to be the starting point for the town . . . inland it should be at the center of the town. The plaza should be square or rectangular, in which case it should have at least one and a half its width for length. . . . (112)

The size of the plaza shall be proportioned to the number of inhabitants taking into consideration the growth the town may experience. [The plaza] shall be not less than two hundred feet wide and three hundred feet long, nor larger than eight hundred feet long and five hundred and thirty-two feet wide. A good proportion is six hundred feet long and four hundred wide. (113)

From the plaza shall begin four principal streets: One [shall be] from the middle of each side and two streets from each corner of the plaza; the four corners of the plaza shall face the four principal winds, because in this manner, the streets running from the plaza will not be exposed to the four principal winds, which would cause much inconvenience. (114)

In the plaza, no lots shall be assigned to private individuals; instead, they shall be used for the buildings of the church and royal houses and for city use, but shops and houses for the merchants should be built first, to which all the settlers of the town shall contribute. . . . (126)

The other building lots shall be distributed by lottery to the settlers . . . and the lots that are left shall be held by us for assignment to those who shall later become settlers. . . . (127)

They shall try as far as possible to have the buildings all of one type for the sake of the beauty of the town. (134)

Cities were built so true to these ordinances that "plaza" and "Mexico" are synonymous. The shaded plaza, often called the *zócalo*, is the heart of the city. A church normally occupies the east side. The rest is circumscribed by arcaded buildings, one of which is the government administrative center.

Mexico City's zócalo, officially named the Plaza de la Constitu-

FIGURE 2.1. Mexico City, Plaza de la Constitución (zócalo).

FIGURE 2.2. Oaxaca City, main plaza (zócalo), west side.

ción, is the largest in the country (Fig. 2.1). The Cathedral, the National Palace, and other fine buildings forming the perimeter seem to be dwarfed by its immensity. Once parklike, today the plaza is paved, used primarily for official functions. Plazas in two of the oldest cities, Tlaxcala and Oaxaca, retain many of their original features. Oaxaca's zócalo exactly fits the precepts of the Ordinances and typifies the colonial city (Fig.2.2). Benches are conveniently located among the trees. Perimeter arcades provide shelter and shade to shoppers. Motor vehicles are not allowed. The plaza is a sanctuary exclusively for people and, except for the quiet mid-afternoon hours, is filled with sounds: the laughter of children, the jocularity of the young, the soft chatter of the adults, the whistles and cries of vendors. The zócalo teems with color and tempting aromas; it is alive! In 1985 UNESCO declared the central core of Oaxaca, long renowned for its colonial ambiance, a World Heritage Site, a place worthy of preservation for future generations.

Tlaxcala became a capital city (of Tlaxcala) by 1524.[2] The government palace (Palacio de Gobierno), constructed after 1545, occupies one full side of the plaza. The building has been considerably altered, but one portal still shows the original design (Fig. 2.3). Three-paneled jambs and a wide lobed arch are filled with deep-cut, heavy floral patterns, a classic example of display architecture meant to impress. The convex curves of the arch, shaped like star points, lend a Moorish accent. The ornamental style is Plateresque but likely executed by a native sculptor. The Plateresque style, then popular in Spain, has a framework of classical equilibrium and compositional clarity within which surfaces are textured with elaborate ornamentation suggestive of silver plate.

Earlier, around 1536 or 1537, the Franciscans had begun construction of their residence (now a museum) and church. The interior of the single nave church measures 49.15 by 11.25 meters, the sanctuary narrowing to 7.85 meters. Spanning the 11-meter nave, a wooden ceiling rises from the walls with two sloping sides connected by a horizontal mid-section (Fig. 2.4). Even though restored, this ceiling remains one of Mexico's most splendid examples of *alfarje* (ceilings of intricately carved and inlaid wood).

Here the Franciscans also constructed a capilla de indios, one of the first open-air chapels in New Spain. Fray Motolinía, the great

FIGURE 2.3. Tlaxcala, government palace, portal.

Franciscan historian, lovingly describes Tlaxcala in his *History of New Spain*, which he wrote from 1536 to 1540 while residing there. His account of the capilla is extensive. He notes that the "chapel of the patio" was completed in 1539, adding, "The chapel has richly carved [*bien labrados*] arches and two choirs, one for the singers and one for those who play instruments. It was all done in six months, and like all the churches they have, it is ornamented and well built."[3]

Today, a three-arched gate looks out upon a steep walk, named "Calle de Capilla Abierta," now enclosed by walls and buildings. One can imagine a large open *atrio* (walled churchyard) sloping down to the west. Some 7 meters behind (east of) the atrio gate is a polygonal structure with three bays, of which the central one juts forward, flanked on both sides by a room (Fig. 2.5). The polygonal section, twice as long as it is wide, is closed with heavy ribs creating a hexagonal chamber, a recessed altar at its rear. Each of its three openings dis-

FIGURE 2.4. Tlaxcala, Franciscan church, alfarje ceiling (Instituto de Investigaciones Estéticas, Universidad Nacional Autónoma de México, México).

FIGURE 2.5. Tlaxcala, Franciscan convento, open-air chapel.

plays a bold ogee arch which is more *mudéjar* (the art of the Moors under Spanish rule) than gothic. A bold cornice, heavy with brackets, ties the whole exterior (about 8 meters in length) together. This must be the capilla described by Motolinía; its arches are indeed "*bien labrados*" and there is space for two choirs. This design for an open-air chapel was not repeated elsewhere.

The bishop's residence from this early period can still be seen in Oaxaca. The red stone used to construct this building is not found in any other structure in the city. Flush with the sidewalk, its single-story facade displays sloping bases surmounted by rectangular panels (Fig. 2.6) much like the *taluds* and *tableros* of Mitla, the nearby prehispanic Zapotec ceremonial center. This facade has long been cited as an example of "Indianism" revival, prevalent in Mexican architecture at the turn of the twentieth century. Astonishingly, this experiment in religious syncretism did not occur in the twentieth century but, according to recent research, in the sixteenth century, most likely in the 1550s. The only serious modification took place in the first

FIGURE 2.6. Oaxaca, former bishop's residence with "taluds and tableros."

decade of the twentieth century. Three windows to the left of the main door were converted into doors. The interior has been extensively modified; however, it is likely the original rooms fronted an inner court much as they now do. Today it is a government building, the Palacio Federal.

"We know a great deal about the conquistadors' houses," writes Toussaint, "about 1554 they seemed like fortresses because of the heaviness of the walls; they were not very high, the lintels and jambs were of cut stone, and over the doors the coats of arms of the owners were displayed; the roofs were flat, of adobe—which around 1581 they began to cover with tile—and they were drained by gutters of wood or terra cotta; the interior arrangement seems to have consisted of a central courtyard surrounded by galleries."[4] Only a few remain. In the 1520s Cortés built a palace in Cuernavaca but only the arched loggias in front and back may be original in the otherwise greatly altered building that today is a museum. His *casa* (home) in Oaxaca has disappeared, but the stone jambs and lintel (of the main door?) may have been preserved as the lower portion of the main entrance to the Museum of Contemporary Art.[5]

The house of Francisco de Montejo, the leading civil authority in Mérida (Yucatán), was built by the Spanish Crown. Its original 1549 facade (Fig. 2.7) remains and, especially in its upper section, exemplifies the Plateresque style. On each side of the lower section freestanding columns flanked by pilasters frame the door. A protruding bracketed cornice creates a clear and strong division. In the upper section diminutive corner figures, virtual finials, are dressed in pelts, their significance something of a mystery. Armored warriors, stepping on Indian heads, guard the Montejo coat of arms. Busts in the upper frieze may represent Francisco, and his wife and son. The interior has been modified for current use by Banamex (a large financial institution) but the front balcony gives evidence that the original structure had two floors. The imposing front, facing the plaza, strongly resembles a church facade. Unquestionably, the sculptor was a Spaniard.

Apart from the conquistadors, among the first of the Spanish settlers to acquire a degree of wealth were shop owners. In Veracruz there is a very early example of a store (*tienda*) fronted by an arcaded walk (Fig. 2.8). This arcade allows the apartment above to have additional depth and privacy. Balconied windows facing the street and doors facing an inner court give good cross ventilation.

FIGURE 2.7.
Mérida, house of
Francisco de
Montejo, portal.

FIGURE 2.8.
Veracruz, store
(lower), residence
(upper).

The Hospital de la Purísima Concepción (now Hospital de Jesús Nazareno) in Mexico City, founded by Hernán Cortés by 1524, is one of the few hospitals that have survived from the sixteenth century.[6] Though modified, it allows some concept of the original. It consists of a church and four sections enclosing two large arcaded courts (Fig. 2.9). On the two floors arcades of a later period enclose large patios; rooms are entered from the covered corridors (Fig. 2.10). In this dual complex one court is for men, the other for women. Flowers, shrubs, trees, and fountains still bring tranquility to the troubled. Another hospital in this city, Amor de Dios, was receiving patients in 1540. Since very early in the sixteenth century every city had a hospital, but these structures were either closed or replaced, mostly in the eighteenth century.

Many large pueblos also had a hospital. Those founded in Michoacán by Bishop Don Vasco de Quiroga and Franciscan friars are famous. These hospitals had a dual function, social as well as medical, which Toussaint describes well.

The hospitals were composed of a great rectangular patio with an open chapel in the center; two of the sides were used for men and for women, respectively, and there were administrative offices on the other sides. But the importance of these hospitals derives less, perhaps, from the architectural structure than from the social organization which they embodied. . . . The hospital was the central office of the organization, for which all the members of the community had to contribute their labor; around it were grouped their houses, which were called *familias* because each one housed a family. There was community land, where everyone was required to work in turn; the produce went to support the hospital and to pay wages to the Indians. . . . The organization of these hospitals . . . was inspired by the famous *Utopia* of St. Thomas More. . . .[7]

Colegios (schools) were another public venture. In New Spain the word originally applied to those institutions devoted to teaching European culture to different age groups. As early as 1525 a colegio was founded in Mexico City for Indian boys. They were taught the basics of literature, arithmetic, Latin, music, singing, and the arts, the classical curriculum. A few years later another was founded for older Indian boys. They were taught religion, writing, Latin composition, rhetoric, and philosophy as well as music, singing, and art. The graduates of this school played a special role in history. They produced

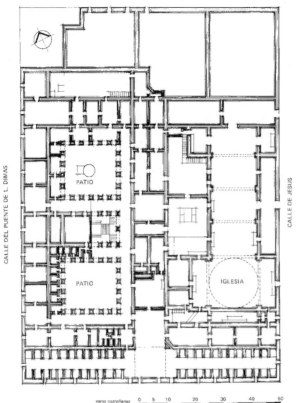

FIGURE 2.9. Mexico City, Hospital de Jesús Nazareno, plan (*Vocabulario arquitectónico ilustrado*, Secretaría del Patrimonio Nacional, México).

FIGURE 2.10. Hospital de Jesús Nazareno, inner patio.

several sixteenth-century Spanish chronicles which provide a lasting account of Mesoamerican culture, practices and beliefs, particularly those of the Aztec world. Before the sixteenth century ended, every city had its colegio. Eventually there were schools to teach Indians and mestizos, boys and girls, criollos, seminarians, orphans, and women. Among the educators, the Franciscans and Jesuits were prominent.

Because students often lived within the confines of the colegio, the plan, by necessity, was extensive yet easy to execute. A module of a patio enclosed on four sides was simply repeated. Long walls rising directly from the sidewalk, two floors high, with many windows in the upper floor but only a few entrances on the lower, typify the exterior.

In approximately 1576 the Jesuits began construction of their colegio in Oaxaca. The complex occupies an entire square block, each side measuring 90 to 95 meters. Some aspects of sixteenth-century workmanship still can be seen in sections of the wall, particularly the coursed stones, the pilasters extending into the second level and ter-

FIGURE 2.11. Oaxaca, Jesuit colegio (calle de Flores Magón).

FIGURE 2.12. Morelia, former Jesuit colegio, now Palacio Clavijero.

minating in scrolls, the string course denoting levels, and the projecting cornice (Fig. 2.11). Classrooms organized around four inner
courts accommodated the three age groups of students (boys). After
the expulsion of the Jesuits (from all of Mexico) in 1767 this school
ceased to function. The complex was then used by another religious
order until about 1890; thereafter the entire place was abandoned for
thirty to forty years. Eventually it was sold piecemeal and the building
was converted to its present use, with stores on the ground level and
dwellings in the upper. With good reason this imposing structure is
locally referred to as "Casa Fuerte."

The former Colegio de la Compañía de Jesús (now Palacio Clavijero) in Morelia, Michoacán, was built in the late sixteenth and early
seventeenth centuries. A long stretch of wall rises directly from the
sidewalk; the church is at the south end of the building (Fig. 2.12).
The single entrance is flanked by many windows. Pedestrians beneath
the windows illustrate how high above ground these windows were
set—not so much for security but to minimize distractions. Without
imparting any particular cadence to the verticals in the facade, the
finials speak for themselves. The entrance received special treatment,

including an axial crest with escutcheon. The main patio is bordered by stately arcades that create covered corridors providing access to rooms. Today the building houses the state public library and tourist office.

At the highest educational level, The Royal and Pontifical University of Mexico was functioning in 1553. On a map of the Plaza de México, dated 1596, the University is depicted in a schematic drawing. If the drawing is accurate, a wide portal was framed by columns topped with a cornice extending beyond the jambs. Over the portal a huge coat of arms, also framed by columns, occupied a space as wide as, yet taller than, the portal. Two escutcheons were set on either side. This central axis is emphasized by a rectangular crest. The entire facade appears Plateresque.

The peoples of Mesoamerica were masters of water conservation and usage. They used terraces and irrigation canals and even practiced a form of hydroponics. The famous gardens of Xochimilco, on the outskirts of Mexico, are filled with *chinampas*, a sort of artificial island made of tree trunks and earth, which still produce an abundance of vegetables and flowers. The natives did not employ the arched aqueduct, however, since the voussoir-keystone principle was not known to their world. Spain, on the other hand, where some of the finest Roman aqueducts are found, had long known that principle. A transfer of such practical architecture to New Spain was natural.

An aqueduct is a striking thing of strength, durability, and beauty. It carries millions of gallons of water great distances. Laying out a route of many miles with a gentle slope equivalent to a drop of one foot per hundred—without a surveyor's theodolite—is no mean engineering feat. The Romans did it and so did the Spanish. With fresh water vital to health and growth, aqueducts were among the first engineering accomplishments of the Spanish settlers.

The water for many colonial cities was supplied by aqueduct. Only vestiges of sixteenth-century structures remain, such as those in Oaxaca, Morelia, and Zacatecas. The aqueduct once servicing Zempoala (Hidalgo) still stands in part. Constructed between 1553 and 1570 under the supervision of the Franciscan Fray Francisco de Tembleque, it was longer and higher than the famous aqueduct in Segovia, Spain. The immense span and height of its arches can still be seen near Otumba pueblo—truly an astounding feat of hydraulic engineering

(Fig. 2.13). Piers of varying heights, erected to a certain level, maintain a constant radius for all arches. Carrying the channel, they march majestically with measured rhythm across the valley for over a half mile.

Fray Tembleque was, of course, familiar with the arch; not so his four hundred native helpers. At first they must have experienced disbelief, even fear. "What holds it up?" they would have wondered. Two hundred years later natives living in the area of today's San Antonio, Texas, might have had the same reaction. In the then frontier settlement of San Antonio, another Franciscan would have overseen the construction of an aqueduct in the 1730s to bring water to the fields of Mission San Francisco de la Espada. Perhaps the oldest functioning aqueduct in the United States, its gently flowing waters are again being used by the National Park Service to irrigate a revitalized mission field.

One of the first military requirements of the Spanish was defense. Forts and walls around Mexico and other inland Spanish cities were considered but not built since the need for them never actually materialized. The real threat came from the sea—buccaneers and pirates. The kings of Spain pursued a vigorous policy of protecting key harbors from which so much wealth from the New World began its journey to Spain. Fortifications were built on the Atlantic and Pacific coasts as well as on the Gulf of Mexico, such as the massive stone fort at Veracruz (Veracruz).

The port of Veracruz was founded in 1519 by Hernán Cortés. During colonial times it was the most important and sheltered harbor in New Spain. Temporary palisades were built almost immediately after the city was founded. These were soon replaced with a masonry fort on an islet, now connected to the mainland by a paved road. It became known as San Juan de Ulúa. In 1590, King Philip II had his military architect, Bautista Antonelli, devise plans for additional fortifications which were executed shortly thereafter. Today this spellbinding gigantic fortress is open to the public.

The fort is built of coral rock surrounded by a moat; a ramp gives access to five bastions and a number of large rooms. Set with a slightly inward slope, outer walls are a good two meters thick at the base and one meter thick at the top (Fig. 2.14). The rounded cornice indicates the level of the flat roof behind the parapet. A watchtower

FIGURE 2.13. Aqueduct near Otumba (Hidalgo).

provides an unobstructed view of both sides. Although the fort is un-questionably utilitarian, the curved molding is distinctive. The pro-portions of the cylindric cupola stand in graceful contrast to the un-remitting forcefulness of the battered wall.

Ammunition was hauled to the roof of the fort by means of a ramp. At its base is a door leading to a cavernous room in which mu-nitions were probably stored. Functionally this entrance could have been shaped like a rectangle, which would have been a simple engi-neering solution. The builder chose instead to add a touch of ele-gance by using a shallow stucco frame, a wide curved cornice, and a small, circular window between cornice and lintel. On the practical side, the ramp, wide enough for a horse-drawn cart or gun, was cor-rugated transversely for increased traction.

Wheeled guns, mounted on the roof behind a splay in the parapet, fitted into a stone channel whose curve determined the arc of fire (Fig. 2.15). Blocks of wood in transverse notches would lock the gun

FIGURE 2.14.
Veracruz, Fort
San Juan de
Ulúa, watch-
tower.

in place. Platforms enabled the soldiers to see over the parapet. The roof was every bit as thick as the wall.[8]

On the Pacific coast, the fort in Acapulco, Guerrero, is quite similar both in layout and history.

During the sixteenth century bishoprics were established and cathedrals begun in seven cities.[9] According to Toussaint, the basilica style was generally favored for these early cathedrals, "the nave [having] a gabled timber roof, and the aisles, flat ceilings on beams."[10] Most of these cathedrals were replaced in the seventeenth century. Only a few other sixteenth-century religious structures in Spanish cities remain intact. One of the most notable is the Dominican church of Santo Domingo in Oaxaca. Well known for the brilliance of its interior decor (seventeenth century), its remarkable architecture is seldom considered.

Santo Domingo is a rectangle, its outer walls enclosing choir, nave, crossing, transepts, and sanctuary with interior measurements of 66 by 22.5 meters. Side chapels extend off the nave. They are interconnected by narrow passageways. Clearly the area normally given to aisles was never designed for processionals nor intended to be occupied by the faithful. The architect transformed the three-aisled basilica into a single nave church. Most likely that architect was Fray Francisco Marín.[11]

The belfried west front measures 27.2 meters in width and even more in height. Set back 2.5 meters from the frontal plane of its tower bases, the four-tiered facade is one-half its width. Its tower-

FIGURE 2.15. Fort San Juan de Ulúa, channel for wheeled gun.

FIGURE 2.16. Oaxaca, Santo Domingo, west front and facade.

facade-tower rhythm of 1 - 2 - 1 makes the west front truly monumental (Fig. 2.16). The church has experienced only three minor alterations: on the south side the Rosary Chapel has been added off the third bay and a new entrance formed out of the sixth bay; on the north side the original entrance into the church from the *convento* through the transept has been closed.

Even though firm construction dates remain elusive, it is certain that Santo Domingo was essentially constructed during the last half of the sixteenth century.[12]

Not enough remains of original sixteenth-century civil architecture in the cities of Nueva España to provide a clear idea of architectural accomplishments and impact. One can try to visualize these low, two-story cities with their large open plazas at the center girded by church, government, and noble family buildings, whose size, location, and Plateresque ornamentation proclaimed their importance. Many city structures were rebuilt, ostensibly because of poor construction, but much pueblo architecture of the sixteenth century survives.

SUGGESTED READING

Cook, Sherburne F., and W. W. Borah. *The Indian Population of Central Mexico, 1531–1610*. University of California Press, 1960.

Crouch, Dora, Daniel Garr, and Axel Mundigo. *Spanish City Planning in North America*. MIT Press, 1982.

Gibson, Charles. *Tlaxcala in the Sixteenth Century*. Yale University Press, 1949.

Toussaint, Manuel. *Colonial Art in Mexico*. University of Texas Press, 1967, Chapter One.

3

Sixteenth Century:
The Formative Era

The Pueblos

For Spain the conversion to Catholicism of the peoples of the Americas was a serious responsibility. Authority to convert the native population was already in the hands of Ferdinand and Isabella, the Catholic monarchs of Spain, by virtue of the Royal Patronage—extensive powers granted by the Popes at the end of the fifteenth century to the Spanish monarchs as Patrons of the Mission Lands. The task of converting the "Indians" was assigned the Franciscans, Augustinians, and Dominicans, commonly known as the religious orders. Pope Paul II in 1537 declared that the Indians were indeed human beings whose human rights were to be respected and who could not be deprived of liberty or property.

Within a short time and with the rapid expansion of the missions, " . . . what was really an extraordinary setup became the ordinary functioning of the Church in the New World; the religious (orders) became strongly entrenched. . . ."[1] The role of the friars (members of the religious orders), who were originally sent as missionaries, was soon enlarged. Their life in the New World was wholly different from their monastic, nonpastoral life in Europe. Priestly prerogatives normally in the hands of the bishops and their priests, the secular clergy, were transferred to the religious orders. In Nueva España, for most of the sixteenth century, friars did not come under the control of the bishop even when assuming the role of parish pastors, remaining responsible only to their Superior. This freedom was reflected in the architecture they created in the sixteenth century, which influenced so much of later building.

Parishes quickly replaced missions. After mid-century secular priests established perhaps more parishes in Nueva España than the Franciscan, Augustinian, and Dominican friars had. Archival sources reveal that in the State of Oaxaca at least 110 pueblo parishes were created between 1538 and 1600, of which almost 75 percent were secular.[2] Each parish and its church was responsible, on average, for five pueblos, most of which also had their own church. By 1600, between 500 and 600 churches existed in Oaxaca. If this regional analysis is extrapolated to the settled areas of Nueva España, then sixteenth-century churches, secular and religious, must have numbered in the thousands. Religious zeal and official policy combined to effect a historic transformation of Mexico.

It was a time without precedent. Historically conversions to Catholicism had been gradual, with the evolution of church architecture following at a measured pace. Never before had the Church been confronted with a situation in which, almost overnight, the number of faithful increased by the tens of thousands. Within fifty years after the arrival of the Spanish friars the peoples of virtually every pueblo in the heartland of Mexico had been baptized—conservatively, ten million converts. It is said that on some days the friar's arm had to be propped up in order for him to continue pouring the baptismal waters. These mass conversions brought in their wake vast architectural needs calling for innovative solutions. This challenge was met by the friars when they devised a new form of architecture unique to the history of European ecclesiastical architecture—the open-air church.

The friars hit upon a novel way of creating imaginary walls which served, in a sense, to define the church. The eastern boundary was delineated by a roofed structure containing the altar where the Mass was said. This represented the sanctuary, or chancel, and generally was the only structural part of the open-air church. Within the walled atrio (churchyard), some 30 to 40 meters from the sanctuary and on its center axis, a cross was set upon a pedestal. This "atrio cross" defined the "west wall" of the imaginary building and in so doing made the north and south walls connecting it to the sanctuary equally imaginable. While the church proper was being built the faithful gathered in their own open-air capilla de indios to hear Mass on Sundays and feast days. Use of the open-air church was never entirely discontinued because the completed church proper simply could not accommodate the throngs of worshippers on major feast days.[3]

So began the process of organizing and constructing the sixteenth-century "convento complex"—not a monastic institution but a parish church with friars in residence. A convento complex often dominated the plaza around which pueblos were normally organized. An architectural pattern used by all three religious orders soon emerged. The sacred site was clearly defined by high walls. Gates provided access to the tranquil, gardenlike enclosed churchyard. The west gate was usually the most important since from it a path led directly to the main entrance of the church, typically located on the far (east) side of the atrio.[4]

In the corners of the atrio were small, open structures called *posas* with two entrances set at right angles and connected by a pathway. Upon leaving the church processions proceeded counterclockwise, stopping at each structure for a short prayer. Hence the name *posa* from the Spanish verb *posar*, meaning to halt. Like the open-air church, posas are unique in Christian architecture. No one has satisfactorily explained their origin. Perhaps the friars realized the importance of outdoor ceremonies to these peoples and wisely assimilated the custom of outdoor worship in a new form.[5]

The west-facing church facade typically rose between heavy tower bases carrying belfries (often only one). This massive west wall was broken only with a single portal, decorated with relief sculpture and, above it, a choir window. In the north nave wall of a number of sixteenth-century convento churches there was another portal even more elaborately decorated, since through it the friar passed on his way to the open-air church to say Mass. At the church's east end was the apse, windowless, often polygonal, at times squared, rarely semicircular.

The interior generally had a single nave with a choir loft at the west and a raised sanctuary at the east end. Midway in each nave wall was a door. The one in the south nave wall led to the friar's residence, the convento. Interior lengths varied considerably, churches longer than 55 meters being categorized as "very large." Width-to-length ratios of single nave churches ranged from the more common 1:4 to 1:5. The high, narrow nave was tunnel-like, usually articulated into four bays. These huge volumes were frequently vaulted, the highest point often more than 10 meters. The raised sanctuary, or chancel, always terminated with a huge altarpiece, the *retablo*, occupying, and often obscuring, the entire apse wall. The retablo was always a prized object with the altar integral to it. Since Vatican II (1963) the altar has been set well out in front of the retablo so the priest may instead face those attending Mass.

Although it normally refers to the residence of the friars, the term convento (often mistakenly translated as convent) can apply to the entire complex (Fig. 3.1). Public entrance to the convento is through the *portería*, a deep, arched portico providing shelter and rest to the waiting visitor. Rooms on the ground level were for offices or communal activities. One of the largest was the refectory with the huge kitchen nearby. When the convento had two floors, individual rooms, or cells, for the friars were found on the upper level, as was the latrine. In the center of the convento was an open area adorned with fruit trees, flowers, and fountains surrounded by a perimeter arcade and covered gallery, known respectively as "cloister court" and "cloister walk."

In terms of architecture the ground plan of the church was certainly the principal contribution of the friar or priest and usually took one of three forms. Most common was the single nave, rectangular church. The infrequently used cruciform plan had a single nave, with bays and transept arms squared to the same dimensions. A surprising number of sixteenth-century churches were basilicas with three aisles. Width-to-length ratios of single-nave churches varied considerably but tended toward either 1:4 or 1:5. The three-aisled church had a 1:3 ratio.

Walls, generally a meter thick, were adobe or *mampostería* (a mixture of stone rubble and cement). Although forms were needed to make the latter type of wall, construction methods were simple and did not require skilled labor. Occasionally wall construction was ashlar. Brick was employed very early, used principally in the construc-

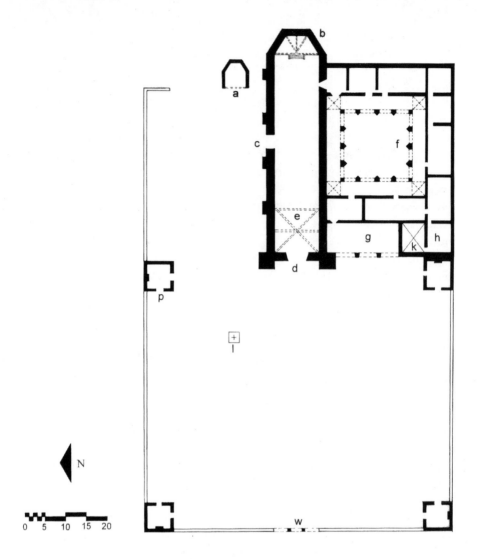

FIGURE 3.1. Plan of ideal convento: **a**, open-air chapel; **b**, apse/vaulted sanctuary; **c**, north door; **d**, facade, main portal; **e**, vault supporting choir; **f**, cloister court; **g**, portería; **h**, kitchen; **k**, herb garden; **l**, atrio cross; **p**, posa; **w**, west atrio gate.

tion of vaults. When vaulting was intended walls were made of mamposterÍa with reinforcing buttresses. Initially naves were covered with a perishable material, often thatch. Sometimes naves were covered with "permanent" wooden ceilings of intricate beauty. Today naves of most sixteenth-century churches are closed with a barrel vault (often concrete). In most sixteenth-century churches the apse was vaulted, normally covering a square about 7 meters to a side. Small windows might have been placed high on the side walls but never in the rear wall, where the entire interior was devoted to the retablo. The apse, housing the sanctuary with its main altar, was often referred to as the *capilla mayor.*

The west end (front) of a sixteenth-century pueblo church was designed as a tall rectangle usually flanked with bell towers, although these often were not constructed until later. The inserted facade was simple in design, often devoid of ornament. When ornamented, a tiered system was employed.

FRANCISCAN CONVENTOS

In 1524, the first group of mendicant missionaries arrived in Nueva España. Known as "the Twelve," they were Franciscans. During the sixteenth century they established no less than 166 conventos among the pueblos of central Mexico, primarily in the states of México, Morelos, Puebla and Michoacán as well as in the outlying states of Campeche and Yucatán. For the next three hundred years members of this order were to perform prodigious feats of conversion and building, founding more conventos and missions than any other religious group. Their accomplishments as friars, writers, teachers, and linguists are equally legendary. They were strong protagonists of the Indians, vigorously defending their rights. Even during the most trying times for the Church, especially the expulsion of the religious orders in 1859, the Franciscans stayed at the insistence of the people.

The arrival of the Franciscans in Nueva España is graphically described by McAndrew.

When the twelve arrived at Tenochtitlán in 1524, Cortés went to welcome them, accompanied by his most important officials and by scores of conquistadors and Indian lords, all carrying wooden crosses. He advanced five hundred paces on his knees, took off his hat, and threw down his cape for fray Martín de Valencia to walk upon, in symbolic imitation of the Entry into Jerusalem on the first Palm Sunday. This of course dramatized for everyone there the Apostolic character of the Twelve and their mission. Kneeling,

Cortés kissed their hands and tried to kiss the cord girdles and hems of their habits without letting the friars bend to him. The other Spaniards followed, and the Indians then imitated the Spaniards, more deeply impressed than they had been by anything since the first appearance of mounted strangers shooting guns. Seeing how deferential mighty Cortés had been to them—Cortés whom many had thought a god or the divine emissary of a god—the Indians realized that the twelve friars must be very, very important, and henceforth spoke to them as they had spoken to their own divine rulers, with hats off and eyes lowered.[6]

CUERNAVACA (Morelos)

One of the earliest Franciscan conventos was founded in Cuernavaca when that community was still a pueblo.[7] The "very large" single-nave church, today a cathedral in the center of the city, was begun in 1529. The date 1552 can be seen on the north portal. Even though the interior has been extensively restored, the original plan and towering meter-thick walls remain, testifying to the church's grandiose

FIGURE 3.2. Cuernavaca, open-air chapel.

scale. Seventeenth-century murals high on the walls depict the martyrdom of forty missionaries in Japan. The modern altar and baptismal font complement the original sober elements. The two-story convento is quite plain with a few preserved murals.

Dating from the 1530s the open-air church, with almost no sculptural decoration, is one of the earliest still standing. Its location is unique, standing at right angles to the church's west wall (Fig. 3.2).[8] Three entry arches, each about 9 by 9 meters, face north, where 50 meters away an atrio cross stands on axis with the central arch. Above the entry arches a layered stone wall rises another 5.5 meters, topped with 28 merlons that are solely decorative. Angled, stepped stone buttresses, as high as the entire wall, counter lateral vault thrusts. Three vaults immediately behind the arches cover areas each about 4.5 meters square. At the south end of the sanctuary three more cover rectangular areas, the center vault ribbed. This vault spans a raised area where an altar once stood. A door in the east bay leads directly to the convento. Cuernavaca's open-air chapel exhibits what may be the first true vaulting in the Americas.

TLALMANALCO (México)

Tlalmanalco's elegance is exceptional among Franciscan establishments. Its grandeur and especially the magnificence of its sculpture give Tlalmanalco's open-air church a unique place in sixteenth-century Mexico. The indigenous date on one of its stones can be interpreted as 1560. It completely overwhelms the adjacent church and convento, not completed until the final decades of the century.

The five entry arches to Tlalmanalco's open-air chapel (Fig. 3.3) span 59.5 meters and give access to an angled wall whose deepest part measures 15.5 meters across. At this point a larger single "triumphal" arch opens to a raised and recessed sanctuary, which was once vaulted and contained an altar. The sculptured arch has three parts—an outer furled design, a "chain" (egg and dart?) in the middle, fauna and faces in the inner ring. The upper part of this arch and its right spandrel are seen (Fig. 3.4) through one of the outer arches (some 15 meters separate the two). Above the keystone, Christ, ruler of the universe, watches from a small niche penetrating an entablature encrusted with dense and deeply sculptured flowers, figures and animals including monkeys in the frames and angels with billowing garments in the spandrels. The angel nearest the arch bears the Franciscan emblem, the stigmata of Saint Francis (the five wounds of Christ). Four wounds are upright "rings," two to a side; the fifth wound, symbolizing the pierced heart of Christ, is a horizontal ring with three nails inserted and blood flowing from each wound.

The triumphal arch is supported by piers that are also profusely carved. On the upper part of the right pier (Fig. 3.5) are a skull and crossbones above two figures, each wearing only a hat and a cloak fastened at the shoulders. Pensively they rest their heads on their hands. In the center of the pier is the face of a man wearing a crown, his raised hands framing his face. Whom is he beseeching, with open mouth and expressive eyes? Below him, on each side, is a serpent's head with large eyes and a curled upper lip touching the arms of the man. From the serpent's neck emerges an odd notched "collar" ending in a spiral. These deeply carved, rounded images (compared to the flat images in the spandrels) evidence the European Renaissance tradition.

The thematic content of the sculpture at Tlalmanaco is perplexing. Rabbits, monkeys, and serpents were not themes of Christian iconography; however, they were symbols sacred in the prehispanic world. Were these creations of a European sculptor influenced by the Mesoamerican world or of an Indian sculptor trained by a European? On the other hand the "blood" of the five wounds and the feathers of the angels' wings are executed in a typically Mesoamerican manner. Of these remarkable reliefs Toussaint says: ". . . while the total effect is Plateresque . . . the character of the sculpture itself is absolutely Indian."[9] This is truly "Mexican" sculpture, a unique blend of European and Mesoamerican cultural traits, one not found elsewhere.

TECAMACHALCO (Puebla)

The immense facade, a solid wall, of this Franciscan church, located a few miles southeast of Puebla City, is pierced only by a door and a choir window (Fig. 3.6). A common design integrates both. The softly lobed ogee arch of the 4.5m-high portal encased in an *alfiz* (rectangle framing the arch) and the draped outer frame give the portal a Moorish accent (Fig. 3.7). Not at all Moorish, however, are the

FIGURE 3.3. Tlalmanalco, open-air chapel with entry arches.

FIGURE 3.4. Tlalmanalco, open-air chapel, detail of arch and spandrel.

FIGURE 3.5. Tlalmanalco, open-air chapel, right pier, upper part.

FIGURE 3.6. Tecamachalco, west front, open-air chapel, convento.

FIGURE 3.7. Tecamachalco, facade, main portal.

FIGURE 3.8. Tecamachalco, stone dated 1590 and 1591 in tower base.

FIGURE 3.9. Tecamachalco, north door with tequítqui relief.

thirteen "flowers" in the frame of the lobed arches nor the "discs" in the alfiz, thirteen on each side of center. (A grouping of thirteen has always been symbolic of the sacred in Mesoamerica.) The roof merlons create the visual effect of balancing the church with the mass of the taller tower.

The warm resonant color of beautifully cut stone surrounding the portal sharply contrasts with the smooth, white stuccoed facade and tower. There are indications that the tower was an addition to the original rectangular facade clearly outlined by a painted "frame." In the tower's base is a stone bearing the Roman numerals "———9, 1590, 1591" (Fig. 3.8). An inscription in Nahuatl reads: "Begun in 1589, completed in 1591." Since interior murals have been identified as the work of Juan Gerson, an Indian born in Tecamachalco, and dated to 1562, the inscribed dates in stone must, therefore, commemorate the completion of the tower, not the church.[10]

A rectangular alfiz also encases the arch of Tecamachalco's north door (Fig. 3.9), the area between filled with perfectly cut light burgundy *tezontle*, a volcanic stone. The frame of the lobed arch is filled with flora in relief, executed in that flat, sharp-edged, two-dimensional manner characteristic of prehispanic sculpture. This sixteenth-century relief sculpture, blending European motifs with Mesoamerican technique, is so distinctive it has been given the name tequítqui. Why this stunning door is located in the north wall when an open-air church lies to the south cannot readily be explained. The latter's sanctuary is on the second story of the entrance to the former convento, located on the same plane as the facade.

FIGURE 3.10. Huejotzingo, atrio cross.

HUEJOTZINGO (Puebla)

Huejotzingo is frequently cited as a model Franciscan convento. Founded between 1524 and 1526, it was completed by 1570. Upon entering the spacious atrio through a magnificent three-arched west gate one sees posas in the four corners. The atrio cross is incredibly beautiful and expressive with nails, exaggerated in size, on each cross arm and on the upright with a crown of thorns at the base (Fig. 3.10).

The church's west front is a tall rectangle of coursed cut stone capped by triangular merlons with angled buttresses at the corners (Fig. 3.11). At midpoint a horizontal passageway modulates its vertical thrust and sets off the top of the facade, a choir window and portal being its principal elements. A cornice and attenuated fluted columns frame the portal. Above the scalloped arch of the door seven discs with the insignia "IHS" (an abbreviation of the Greek word for Jesus) project boldly.

FIGURE 3.11. Huejotzingo, west front.

FIGURE 3.12. Huejotzingo, choir window.

The arched and splayed choir window (Fig. 3.12) is girded with a carved Franciscan cord studded with nine knots. (The Franciscan habit has a cincture at the waist. If the friar belongs to the First Order, his cincture has three knots, representing the three vows he takes. If the friar belongs to the Third Order, his cincture carries five knots, representing the Five Wounds of Christ.) Flanking the choir window are the stigmata of Saint Francis depicting the five wounds he bore, likewise encircled with a nine-knot Franciscan cord (Fig. 3.13). The almost congealed "blood" flowing from the five wounds

FIGURE 3.13. Huejotzingo, escutcheon flanking choir window with stigmata.

FIGURE 3.14.
Huejotzingo,
posa.

FIGURE 3.15
(opposite page).
Huejotzingo,
view of nave
looking toward
sanctuary.

is Mesoamerican in depiction. Why the unfamiliar image of nine knots? These could refer to the Nine Lords of the Underworld, a symbol of death in the prehispanic world. By using symbols of the sacred familiar to the people of his pueblo the sculptor imparted the significance of the new creed surrounding Christ's passion and death. These superb works of relief sculpture are classic examples of tequítqui.

Huejotzingo's posas are square stone structures about 3 meters long and 4.5 meters high with two arched openings and capped with a pyramid of stone. A doorway in the posa in the southwest corner is framed with a nine-knotted Franciscan cord flowing around the arches (Fig. 3.14). In the spandrels winged angels carry instruments of Christ's passion above which are Franciscan emblems (stigmata), four on each side. One could convincingly argue that the same native sculptor also created those designs flanking the choir window.

FIGURE 3.16. Huejotzingo, retablo (Instituto de Investigaciones Estéticas, Universidad Nacional Autónoma de México, México).

Huejotzingo is another "very large" church, its interior measuring 62 by 15.5 meters (203 x 50 feet). It consists of a single nave terminating in a polygonal apse. High nave walls run unbroken giving a dark tunnel effect, "lighted" at the far end by the sanctuary (Fig. 3.15). The four nave vaults and that closing the sanctuary are ribbed. Today the entire complex is designated a Colonial Monument and used as a museum.

The screenlike retablo (Fig. 3.16) filling the east wall is among the very few remaining sixteenth-century gilded wooden altarpieces, complete with free-standing statues, reliefs, and colorful oil paintings. Its division into four horizontal tiers and seven vertical sections is clearly defined by the polychrome frame. Fourteen gilded statues of saints, all of museum quality, stand in the niches framed by pairs of columns and entablatures. Constructed under the guidance of an *ensamblador*, the retablo represents the work of several guilds: carpenter, wood carver, joiner, sculptor, gilder, and painter. The paintings were signed by the Flemish painter Simón Pereyns and dated 1586.

AUGUSTINIAN CONVENTOS

The Augustinians were active in the States of México, Morelos, Hidalgo and Michoacán. Their establishments number among the most elaborate and ornate of the conventos built by the three religious orders. Architecturally Augustinian complexes were generally the most "correct," i.e., they most closely followed one of several European "just published" architectural treatises. This is particularly exemplified by the sculptured church facades. The *espadaña*, or pierced belfry, rising abruptly above the west face is often associated with Augustinian churches.

FIGURE 3.17. Acolman, church, open-air chapel, convento.

FIGURE 3.18. Acolman, atrio cross.

ACOLMAN (México)

The sumptuous ashlar stonework of Acolman's church facade contrasts strikingly with the starkness of the rest of its west front, which has the characteristic espadaña (Fig. 3.17). This tall rectangular facade was added in 1560 to the already twenty-year-old church. A strong cornice holds tautly a lower flat rectangle filled by paired columns, statues, and an arched door. Between this cornice and an equally strong upper one a square is formed containing an arched choir window flanked with Augustinian escutcheons.

The long, two-story rough-faced stone structure to the south is the convento, with five arches indicating the portería. On the second floor, sandwiched between the church and the convento, is a deeply shadowed opening with an alfiz frame. This is the sanctuary of the open-air church. From the sanctuary to the cross at the west end of the atrio the ground slopes gently upward; a friar saying Mass or preaching would have been easily seen or heard. The unusual atrio cross (Fig. 3.18) has a finely detailed Renaissance-style head of Christ at the intersection, "flames" jutting from the ends of floral-patterned cross arms, instruments of the Passion on the upright, and a tequítqui relief of the Virgin at the base.

The facade, honoring Saint Peter and Saint Paul, is steeped in the Spanish tradition of the Plateresque (Fig. 3.19). Yet there are taunting hints of a tradition not European. Toussaint notes that while "the form itself is European, the technique and even the motifs of the ornament are Indian."[11] Both saints exhibit the hallmark realism of Renaissance sculpture, exemplified by Saint Peter's convincing corporeal weight, posture, attire, and a face filled with solemn intensity (Fig. 3.20). The paired classic columns carry Ionic capitals and fluted shafts. But there is something distinctive about the "swags of cloth" encircling the shafts since they are not standard repertoire in Renaissance ornamental sculpture. Also unusual are the swag "knots" with open loops and trailing ends. Similar knots appear frequently in Mesoamerican sculpture, murals, and códices (illuminated manuscripts). Exalted persons are often shown wearing headdresses secured by a soft material with an open loop and trailing ends.[12] Presumably the European-trained sculptor of Acolman's facade had several very capable Mesoamerican assistants producing a subtle blending of the "old" sacred with the "new."

FIGURE 3.19. Acolman, church facade.

FIGURE 3.20. Acolman, facade, detail, statue of Saint Peter.

FIGURE 3.21. Acolman, apse closed with rib vault.

The single nave of the church is an immense unbroken volume, running 60 meters from the west door to the sanctuary retablo. Its 12-meter width creates a tunnel effect somewhat dampened by low groined nave vaults which contrast sharply with the complex rib vault of the polygonal apse (Fig. 3.21). In the sanctuary are some of Acolman's best preserved murals depicting Augustinian heroes; bishops, cardinals and popes are seated on magnificent thrones.

METZTITLÁN (Hidalgo)

The west front of this Augustinian church, begun in the 1540s, is an unforgettable sheer unbroken plane (Fig. 3.22). The deep shadows of the portal and choir window are the only intrusions into the otherwise solid rectangular mass. The strongly vertical facade is tempered by two horizontal bands, the shorter one over the portal and another stretching across the top. Light diffused openings mark the seven bells in the espadaña. A small atrio cross is set upon a large pedestal.

The facade follows that of Acolman but lacks the latter's unified design and proportions. The choir window sits high and seems disjointed from the portal; both window and portal are relatively narrow. The overall effect is that of a series of unrelated parts. Perhaps this lack of understanding of classical design is what is so eye-catching. Statues, as lifelike as those at Acolman, are similarly set between paired columns with knotted swags tied around them (Fig. 3.23).

Recessed behind the plane of the west front, the two-story convento has a three-arched portería. In the peaceful cloister court the lower-level arches are notably graceful with their multiple moldings (Fig. 3.24). Buttresses support a vaulted cloister walk. Second-floor arches are simpler, appearing much smaller, an effect created by the seamless balustrade and its contoured top running the entire circuit of the cloister court. All walls are stone, each piece beautifully cut. The geometric patterns of the murals covering the barrel vaults of the

FIGURE 3.22. Metztitlán, west front.

FIGURE 3.23. Metztitlán, church facade, detail, statue.

FIGURE 3.24.
Metztitlán, cloister
court.

cloister walk are among the brightest and most vigorous remaining from the sixteenth century.

Metztitlán's single-nave church, containing some fine retablos and murals, is laid out on an unusual north-south axis, likely occasioned by topography. The complex overlooks a deep canyon which bisects the pueblo, one of the most attractive and untouched in Mexico.

YECAPIXTLA (Morelos)

San Juan Bautista, Yecapixtla, founded between 1535 and 1540, seems untouched by time. A merloned wall girdles the complex. Steps lead up to its west gate, high above the present street level, opens upon a large (111 by 106 meters) shaded atrio. A glance to either side reveals corner posas so carefully maintained they look new, even to the recessed altars. Straight ahead a tree-lined path with an atrio cross stretches toward a majestic gabled west front with a merloned crest. Instead of an espadaña, a large bell tower is to the south, set behind the plane of the facade (Fig. 3.25).

Angled at 45 degrees, buttresses cradle an ornamented facade replete with some of the finest Plateresque sculpture in Mexico. An entablature and paired fluted half-columns frame an elegant portal (Fig. 3.26). Reliefs are refined, expertly articulated. A panel just above the entablature depicts the symbols of the Franciscan Order (at right) and the Augustinian Order (at left). The latter (Fig. 3.27) represents the pierced heart of Christ surmounted by a cardinal's hat (as worn by Saint Augustine, a doctor of the Church). The center niche may never have held a statue. In the pediment, Christ crucified is fully carved, a rare iconograph on a sixteenth-century facade. A large circu-

FIGURE 3.25.
Yecapixtla, view from
atrio gate to west front
of church.

FIGURE 3.26. Yecapixtla, facade and main portal.

FIGURE 3.27. Yecapixtla, symbol of Augustinian Order.

lar choir window (*óculo*) displays open gothic tracery whose delicacy rivals that of any in Spain (Fig. 3.28). The north portal has sculptured reliefs of similar quality. Black and white heraldic murals on the lower choir walls are remarkably fresh and vibrant.

YURIRIA (Guanajuato)

The Augustinian complex in Yuriria, erected between 1550 and 1567, ranks among the largest in Mexico. Although the identity of convento architects is rarely known, the architect for this complex is. He, Pedro del Toro, left a portrait of his wife and himself sculptured on the portería. The atrio has disappeared but a parklike setting emphasizes the grandioseness of the complex (Fig. 3.29). Anchored by a gigantic bell tower, placed forward, the church facade occupies al-

FIGURE 3.28. Yecapixtla, choir window (óculo).

FIGURE 3.29. Yuriria, west and south sides of complex.

most the entire west front. Four tall, narrow arches announce the
portería and the adjoining two-story convento.

The Plateresque facade, set between slight projections, is lavish
(Fig. 3.30). It is an assemblage of four tiers, each distinctively pat-
terned. The lowest zone is a clear copy of Acolman's Saints Peter and
Paul framed between ornate columns (Fig. 3.31). Their verticals are
emphasized by four Atlantean figures in the second tier. Diminutive
musicians, playing and singing with gusto, grace the three small
niches in this zone otherwise filled with a swirling pattern (Fig. 3.32).
The óculo in the third tier is wedged between two huge panels festooned with leafy garlands. A figure with mitre and staff, probably the

FIGURE 3.30.
Yuriria, church
facade.

patron Saint Augustine, stands in a niche in the fourth tier with tendrils gracefully curving toward the center.

The "very large" single-nave cruciform church terminates in a heavily buttressed semicircular apse. Merlons line the entire parapet in an unbroken series. Barrel vaulting in the nave is coffered. Ribbed vaults close the transepts, sanctuary, and cloister walks.

DOMINICAN CONVENTOS

The Dominicans made Oaxaca State "their" territory. After a brief but highly successful missionary effort in Oaxaca, they established their first permanent residence in 1538. Before the century ended more than twenty conventos had been founded, many recognized as among the finest examples of sixteenth-century architecture in Mexico.

TEPOSCOLULA (Oaxaca)

San Pedro y San Pablo, Teposcolula, was "accepted" by the Dominicans in 1538.[13] Originally the church had a single nave, 47 meters long and 11 meters wide. In 1692, it was transformed into a cruciform church and lengthened to 64.5 meters.[14] During this enlargement campaign the domical vaults closing the four bays were probably constructed.

Intriguing figures in the tower bases face four to the front and four to the facade. A female saint (Fig. 3.33) appears free-standing but is actually "engaged," sculptured in place. Particularly fascinating are the "Ionic" pedestals at the base of the statues. In one, a fearsome face is more akin to a deity figure in a Mixtec codex than a Western angelic image (Fig. 3.34). What could the native artist have known about Ionic capitals, about Christian angels, represented as humans with feathered wings? Only what he was shown—a small woodcut. He would have readily understood the need for symbols—his world was full of them, especially feathers when associated with the Feathered Serpent. Why not then carve the "Ionic capital" with feathers, thereby proclaiming to his fellow citizens its "sacredness"? This creation by a native sculptor is a blending of two cultures and one of the earliest examples of tequítqui in Nueva España.

FIGURE 3.31. Yuriria, facade, detail, statue of Saint Peter.

FIGURE 3.32. Yuriria, facade, detail, second tier, musicians.

FIGURE 3.33.
Teposcolula, church fa-
cade, detail, female saint.

FIGURE 3.34.
Teposcolula, facade, de-
tail, pedestal with "Ionic"
capital, tequítqui relief.

FIGURE 3.35 (opposite
page). Teposcolula, open-
air chapel, church, con-
vento (on far right).

The glory of Teposcolula is its open-air chapel. "No more skillful vault had been built in the Americas. It was perhaps the finest example in the New World of medieval craftsmanship on a grand scale which survived to our time."[15] This diaphanous structure (Fig. 3.35) is 43 meters long, 11 meters deep. The "facade" consists of five arches, the rear "bay" has six. A hexagonal vault in the center, mostly collapsed, unified the entire design. Radial thrusts are met with four buttresses set diagonally, the forward ones projecting well beyond the plane of the outer arcade. The rear wall once held a retablo and altar; the raised platform is still present. This masterpiece, started in 1549 and completed by 1555, is one of several works by the Dominican architect Fray Francisco Marín and deservedly classified a Colonial Monument.

Why construct such an elaborate open-air church more than ten years after founding San Pedro y San Pablo? This was by far the largest and most ornate open-air church in Nueva España. Begun soon after Yanhuitlán's church of Santo Domingo was started this monumental structure possibly was a "peace offering" to the peoples of Teposcolula jealous of their arch-rivals in Yanhuitlán.

The two-story convento has overall dimensions of 47 by 33 meters. The open court (19 by 19) is surrounded by four arched bays to a side, the barrel vault of its walk bolstered by squared buttresses. The portería (9.5 by 9.5) is entered through two arcades with tequítqui designs.

YANHUITLÁN (Oaxaca)

The Dominicans formally assumed responsibility for the spiritual welfare of Yanhuitlán and its many dependencies in 1548, beginning the church of Santo Domingo that same year. It is one of the glories of sixteenth-century Mexican architecture.

Church and convento are situated upon elevated terrain. This immense "platform" (Fig. 3.36) is clearly manmade, much of it raised three to five meters, suggesting it previously served as a base of a prehispanic temple. The complex is staggering in size, covering 24,000 square meters. The atrio, to the north of the church, measures 120 by 90 meters. It then extends 35 meters to the west of the facade, where a flight of 28 balustered steps, 6.5 meters wide, connects with the road.

Made entirely of dressed masonry, the exterior of the church measures 79 meters in length, 17.5 in width and 25 in height. The north

FIGURE 3.36. Yanhuitlán, plan, with "platform" and complex.

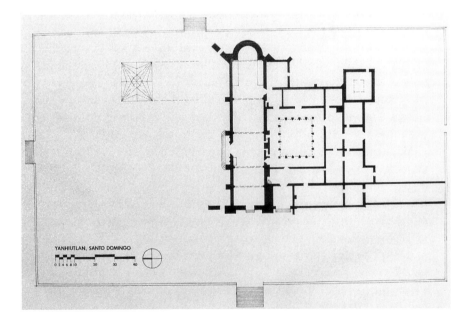

YANHIUTLAN, SANTO DOMINGO

0 2 4 6 8 10 20 30 40

nave wall (Fig. 3.37) is windowless; two massive arched buttresses were later added. A string course, girding the entire structure except the facade, marks the spring of the vaults. Resting on this sill, four "round-headed" windows are centered between five buttresses. A handsomely sculpted portal occupies the entire second bay (Fig. 3.38). Its upper portion consists of pedestals and finials, extensions of the portal's outer frames, from which a curved border of stone reaches to the verticals announcing the "gothic" window. This elaborate north door, a splendid example of the Plateresque, is one of the finest in Mexico.

The west front extends 24 meters with the facade set slightly recessed between tower bases (Fig. 3.39). Each part of the three-by-three facade is clearly delineated, but the progression of the classical orders from lowest tier to the top is unusual—Doric, Corinthian and Ionic. The mixtilinear crest is most likely a later addition. This serene Renaissance facade is quite different from the Plateresque north portal. It displays a hand well-attuned to the new restrained, clearly articulated structural style of the Renaissance, which "began to make itself felt in Mexico about 1570."[16] In 1975 it was discovered that an original facade with a circular choir window lies beneath this Renaissance facade.[17] The original main door with coffered diamonds like those on the north door can still be seen on its intrados. The monumental semi-circular apse (Fig. 3.40) is a masterpiece of masonry without an equal in all of colonial Mexico.

The single nave is an imposing volume measuring 74.5 meters in length, 14.5 in width and 26 in height (Fig. 3.41). The division of the nave into four bays is subtle. Only at the juncture of bays three and four does an engaged column rise from floor to spring. Each stone nave vault is supported by a complex pattern of ribs, tied together by a central octagonal wheel (Fig. 3.42). The pointed 15-meter transverse rib and the radial 23-meter diagonal rib result in a domical vault. The friars undoubtedly wanted the interior to resemble that of a church in Spain where ribbed vaulting was used well into the sixteenth century. What held up the stone vaults would have been both inexplicable and mysterious to the people of Yanhuitlán, who never before had seen an enclosed space larger than the interiors of their small homes.

A triumphal arch, richly sculptured, announces the sanctuary. Its

FIGURE 3.37.
Yanhuitlán,
north nave wall.

FIGURE 3.38.
Yanhuitlán,
north door in
second bay of
nave wall.

FIGURE 3.39. Yanhuitlán, west front.

FIGURE 3.40. Yanhuitlán, apse, semicircular.

first six meters are closed with a coffered barrel vault and the last three with a ribbed and coffered semicircular vault. Filling the east wall is a magnificent retablo, the work of Andrés de Concha. Since the contract for the retablo was signed around 1568–1570 the apse must have been closed by the early 1570s.[18]

On the south side of the church the convento measures 56 by 47 meters. The 18.5-by-16 cloister court is surrounded by vaulted walks, each side having five arched bays separated by prow-shaped buttresses. Offices and community rooms once comprised the lower floor, accessed from a portería nine meters square. No less than sixteen cells, all of brick, were on the second floor, as was the large latrine.

FIGURE 3.41. Yanhuitlán, view from mid-nave toward sanctuary.

FIGURE 3.42. Yanhuitlán, ribs of nave stone vault.

A meeting of the whole Dominican province was held at Santo Domingo in January 1558. Perhaps as many as fifty friars attended, so the convento must have been completed to a stage where this large number of friars could have been accommodated and religious services conducted. Temporary roofing could have made Santo Domingo suitable for holding religious services. The north portal must also have been completed, since church construction in sixteenth-century Mexico routinely included the portals when nave walls were erected.

The Dominican chronicler Francisco de Burgoa, writing in the 1660s, said Santo Domingo took 25 years to complete and that an architect was involved, but he gave no name.[19] Another Dominican, Dávila Padilla, described Fray Francisco Marín as one who, "with the skill of an architect, drew plans for the community's churches and conventos and supervised their construction."[20] The official records show that Fray Marín had many assignments in a few years, a highly unusual occurrence for a Dominican friar. He was assigned to Yanhuitlán in 1550. It can be inferred that Fray Marín was the architect of Santo Domingo.[21]

Among the many details distinguishing Yanhuitlán is the superb craftsmanship seen everywhere. Church walls—interior and exterior—and even the exterior walls of the convento are precisely cut ashlars. North portal and curved apse are without equal. The nave's length-to-width ratio of 1:5 fits the precepts for single-nave churches expounded by Rodrigo Gil de Hontañón, the great Spanish sixteenth-century theoretician. His structural rule for buttress thickness, that its depth measured from the church interior to the outermost buttress surface should be one-fourth the span, is followed at Yanhuitlán where the depth of the buttress is 3.8 meters and the span is 14.5.[22]

CUILAPAN (Oaxaca)

In 1550 the Dominican Order officially assumed responsibility for serving the Mixtecs of Cuilapan, then the largest community in the Valley of Oaxaca. Santiago, Cuilapan, as seen today had its origins in that decade. Six major parts make up the very large (236 by 114 meters) complex (Fig. 3.43). From north to south: a three-aisled capilla de indios (70 by 20), a four-bay church (60 by 17), a detached belfry

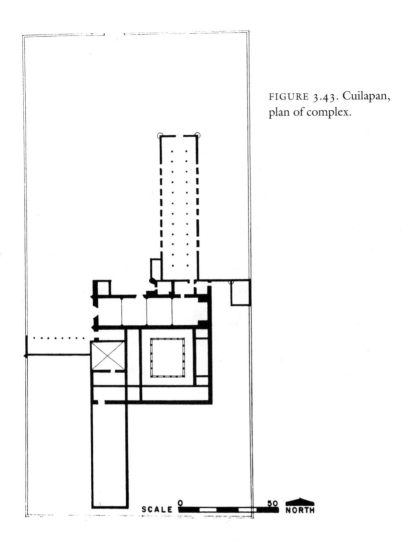

FIGURE 3.43. Cuilapan, plan of complex.

SCALE 0 50 NORTH

against the east perimeter wall, a two-storied convento (58 by 38), a large portería (34 by 7), and a long rectangular wing attached to the south of the convento.

To the north of the three-aisled capilla a small atrio cross is mounted on a large base (Fig. 3.44). Over the central arch of the tower-flanked facade are the remains of an end wall which, presumably, once supported a gabled roof. Passing through the central arch, long arcades form a (roofless) nave and aisles. The view down the nave ends abruptly in a wall (Fig. 3.45) erected in 1920 creating a chapel "inside" the church, but destroying the rhythmic flow of

FIGURE 3.44. Cuilapan, atrio cross, three-aisled open-air chapel.

arches to what was the rib-vaulted sanctuary. The original configuration of nave, triumphal arch, and sanctuary is shown in the plan (Fig. 3.46). A sixteenth-century mural in the sacristy shows the structure with a tiled, gabled roof and four corner towers.[23] The eighteen entrances in the nave walls, plus the three in the facade, would have made it an "open-air" church even when roofed.[24] In the wall terminating the west aisle is a stone set about two meters off the floor, inscribed with the date 1555 and its corollary date in Mixtec, probably commemorating the capilla's completion.

The north wall of the church of Santiago rises perpendicular to, and twice the height of, those of the open-air chapel. The two structures abut at the bay nearest the apse. The single nave with four bays terminates in a narrowed shallow apse housing the sanctuary. Litigation over Cortés's estate, of which Cuilapan was a part, stopped work around 1580. Eventually (possibly in 1777), the two eastern nave bays were closed with domical vaults. The fountain of ribs seen in the upper level of the nave walls testifies to intended rib vaults (Fig. 3.47). Had the nave been completed as planned it would have matched the four-bay interior of Yanhuitlán with its ribbed vaults and undelineated nave.

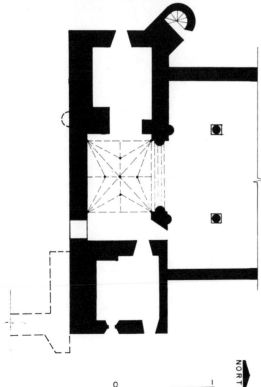

FIGURE 3.45. Cuilapan, open-air chapel, south terminus of nave.

FIGURE 3.46. Cuilapan, original configuration of sanctuary in open-air chapel.

SCALE 0 ___ 1

NORTH

The west end of the church displays unusual features (Fig. 3.48). Flanking paired columns and a dentiled pediment suggest a classical design. Are the capitals within the pediment tilted because the (native?) sculptor had no concept of the classic capital and its function, or because the designer wanted to maintain the solid line of dentils at

FIGURE 3.47. Cuilapan, main church, ribs of unfinished nave vault; "Dominican" corbel.

any cost? Also distinctive are the two choir windows, instead of the usual single window.

Both the location of the (roofless) portería, set at a right angle to the convento entrance, and its nine arches are unusual.[25] The north convento wall is also the south nave wall of the church. This wall is so thick (almost three meters) it "conceals" buttresses, confessionals and stairways. The entrance to the church from the convento is a veritable tunnel. In the corners of the cloister walk are murals which Burgoa described as having been "painted by an Indian." A large kitchen looks directly out upon a herb garden. On the second floor there were originally at least sixteen cells. Santiago Cuilapan was always, therefore, intended to serve as more than just a residence for the small number (four to six) of assigned friars. This expectation was fulfilled in October 1578, when a meeting of the Dominican Province took place there.

In retrospect, Santiago Cuilapan may reflect failed experimentation. It is the only Dominican complex in Mexico with a roofed open-air church, a capilla attached to the main church, and a portería jutting out at right angles to the convento.

FIGURE 3.48. Cuilapan, main church, west front, facade.

SECULAR CHURCHES

If the number of secular churches exceeded those of the religious clergy, no secular church is known to have achieved the monumentality of that in Huejotzingo, Acolman, or Yanhuitlán. The secular clergy simply could not match the religious clergy in resources. Architectural construction methods, however, were much the same. The quarters needed for one or two priests never reached the size of a convento designed for a number of friars. Although posas are nominally associated with sixteenth-century complexes of the three religious orders, they were common among the church atrios created by the secular clergy. The processional posa remains a constant, living tradition.

MITLA (Oaxaca)

When the Spanish arrived in Oaxaca in 1521 there was no native religious center in that region which could match Mitla either in significance or size. In 1544, the secular pastor assigned to Mitla established the parish church, San Pablo, still functioning as such today. The church is centered on the east side of a 32-by-42-meter paved atrio with a refurbished posa in each corner. The facade's metope/triglyph entablatures and sober design speak eloquently of a nineteenth-century neoclassic "remodeling."

The church exterior traverses 39 meters in length, 12 in width. Three nave bays (9.5 by 9.5) are closed with lanterned octagonal domes. Construction of these vaults took place perhaps as late as the nineteenth century. Mitla's squared apse, closed with a hemispherical dome with cupola, has a width and height considerably less than those of the nave and is likely sixteenth century. Behind it a larger and more recent octagonal dome closes the bay nearest the sanctuary in an attempt to create a stately crossing dome; another covers the choir.

The south atrio wall was part of a prehispanic structure and displays a fretted geometric pattern (*greca*) characteristic of Mitla, consisting of four rows, two descending and two ascending (Fig. 3.49). Each row terminates in a "hook," thirteen to a row, for a total of fifty-two. These numbers were not fortuitous. In this foremost Zapotec religious center, the numbers thirteen and fifty-two were fre-

FIGURE 3.49. Mitla, south atrio wall.

quently displayed sacred symbols, and are still visible on other prehispanic structures at Mitla.

HUAUTLA (Oaxaca)

San Miguel Huautla was a secular parish in 1564. Today the pueblo sits on the near embankment, the church across the river. The walled atrio is notably lower than the church (Fig. 3.50). Considerable work must have been required to level the area, measuring 41 meters in the north-south axis and 38 in the east-west. Centered on the axis of the church is a small wooden atrio cross set upon a stone pedestal. The west wall of the church is a single plane flanked by buttresses set at a 45-degree angle. To the north, the belfry is a separate structure. A gabled, timbered and tiled roof covers the rectangular nave (39.5 by 7.5 meters); buttresses indicate intended, but never executed, vaulting.

FIGURE 3.50. Huautla, view of west front from atrio.

The facade, a masterpiece of tequítqui, has an alfiz frame filled with what appears to be a corn stalk entwined with a serpent. The star-shaped door, made of three large voussoirs, and choir window with its ogee arch are adorned with blossoms. The center facade relief depicts Saint Peter (Fig. 3.51) seated and crowned (with a tiara?), holding

symbolic keys. Garments are carved in flat relief. Uprights framing
Saint Peter are etched with what appear to be feathers. In the base a
bird with a long beak and a snarling jaguar are depicted. On each side
a relief cross is surrounded by bead-like clusters, framed with twisted,
knotted cords.

San Miguel has a remarkable and well-preserved sixteenth-century
facade. It displays an extraordinary number of symbols sacred to the
prehispanic world. The most obvious is the serpent. Throughout
Mesoamerica the corn stalk was universally associated with the maize
deity. The feline, particularly the jaguar, and feathers were also univer-
sal symbols of the sacred. The "bead-like clusters" are much like
blood portrayed in prehispanic representations of sacral offerings.

FIGURE 3.51. Huautla, facade, detail, portal with alfiz, tequítqui reliefs.

ARCHITECTS AND FRAY FRANCISCO MARÍN

Perhaps a few architects designed sixteenth-century pueblo secular churches, but for the most part that was the pastor's task. Whether priest or friar his "architectural training" consisted of becoming familiar with a few principles: ratio of length to width; thickness and height of walls; materials for walls and roofing; the place to begin. His resources were native artisans, unfamiliar with European practices.

The cathedrals tell a different story. A number of architects are associated with the sixteenth-century cathedrals of Nueva España.[26] A few others have been identified as architects of religious complexes. Toussaint names seven architects of the many sixteenth-century Franciscan conventos, four of whom were friars. For the Augustinian conventos he names three architects, of whom two were priests, but he names only one, a friar, for the Dominican conventos.[27] Now a second name can be added, Fray Francisco Marín.

What is known about the Dominican priest, Fray Francisco Marín? Only two salient facts: first, that he was an architect (see note 20); second, that he was a very busy friar.

A review of the official records, the *actas* (see note 13), of the periodic chapter meetings held by the Dominicans of the Province of Santiago, Mexico, shows that a certain friar had, within a fifteen-year period, nine assignments. This was highly unusual since assignments to a pueblo as a parish priest were normally for a long time, sometimes for life. Furthermore, these nine assignments between 1541 and 1556 were closely linked to other church-related events sufficiently significant to the Province to be recorded in the actas.[28] This "certain friar" was none other than Fray Francisco Marín. What was this peripatetic friar doing? Evidently "drawing up plans of churches and overseeing their execution." Of immediate interest is the fact that in a four-year span—between 1546 and 1550—Fray Francisco was assigned to three places: Yanhuitlán (1550–1552), Coixtlahuaca (1546–1547) and Oaxaca (1547–1548).

Yanhuitlán

The architectural characteristics of Santiago Yanhuitlán were detailed earlier.

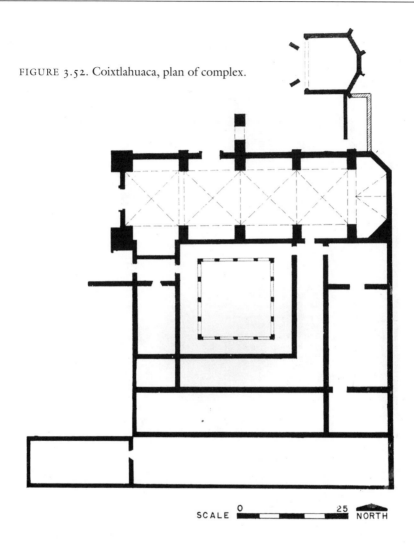

FIGURE 3.52. Coixtlahuaca, plan of complex.

SCALE 0 25 NORTH

Coixtlahuaca

San Juan Bautista Coixtlahuaca was far enough along in its construction of church and convento that a provincial meeting could be held
there in 1564.

In plan (Fig. 3.52) San Juan is a single-nave church with four bays
and a polygonal apse. An open-air chapel is to the north, the con-

FIGURE 3.53. Coixtlahuaca, view of nave looking toward sanctuary.

vento to the south. Measurements are impressive: the church is 63 by 20 meters; the convento, mostly in ruins, is 54 by 55; the facade occupies 12.8 meters of the 22-meter west front. It is dated 1576, completed some 28 years after church construction had begun.

The four-bay nave terminates in an elevated sanctuary which lacks the usual triumphal arch (Fig. 3.53). Domical five-ribbed star vaults close each of the four bays. Even in their weak definition there are parallels to Santo Domingo in Yanhuitlán. Only in the fourth bay, that adjoining the sanctuary, does a flat pier reach from floor to spring. At the other bays "extruded" corbels, descending to the level of spring of the barrel vaults closing the chapels, carry the sprout of nine ribs. Only the second and fourth bays have wheel ribs at their apex. The first and third terminate in a large boss.

At eye-level only the bay nearest the sanctuary is defined to ground level. In this respect the naves of Yanhuitlán and Coixtlahuaca are quite similar.[29] However, unlike Yanhuitlán, each bay is flanked by a niche, 2.4 meters deep and 11.9 meters long. The arcaded nave openings have the same 11.9-meter span. These "chapels," formed by interiorized buttresses, are not interconnected. Each is closed with a barrel vault whose axis is perpendicular to the nave. As in Yanhuitlán a vaulted choir loft occupies the first bay. Against the 61-meter length of the interior, the 13-meter width of the nave proper creates a ratio of 1:4.7. A gilt retablo virtually conceals the shape of the solid ashlar polygonal apse but above it twelve ribs and vaulting, forming the apse closure, are visible.

Santo Domingo, Oaxaca

A close view of the plan of Santo Domingo in the city of Oaxaca (Fig. 3.54) shows it to be a solid rectangle enclosing choir, nave, side chapels, crossing, transepts, and sanctuary. The interior measurements, from wall to wall, are 66 by 22.5, a ratio of 1:2.9. However, the lateral chapels are effectively concealed by piers and screens.

The nave (Fig. 3.55) is organized into six rectangular bays, the choir occupying the first two. Every two bays form a square of 13.2 by 13.2. Each nave bay is then divided by a small arch into two rectangles of 6.5 by 13.2. This same 13.2-by-13.2 unit is found in the sanctuary. Given this nave width the ratio now becomes 1:5, the "classic" ratio for single-nave churches.

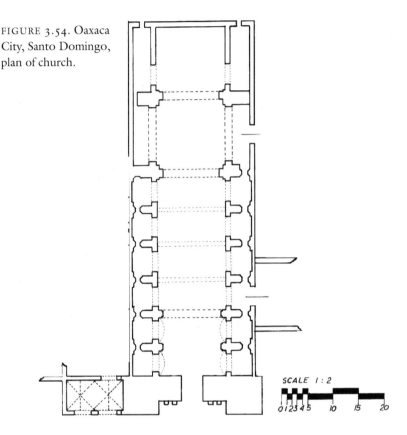

FIGURE 3.54. Oaxaca City, Santo Domingo, plan of church.

SCALE 1 : 2

0 1 2 3 4 5   10   15   20

The crossing and transepts presented serious technical problems during construction. The depth of the transept was restricted by the coterminus convento wall and could not, therefore, reach the ideal "one-half width of the nave."[30] Furthermore, the crossing, by definition a square, had to be larger than the rectangle of the nave bay. To create a square the centers of the crossing piers were set at 14.5 meters.

The base circumference of the crossing vault extends beyond the plane of the crossing square. Hence there is no drum. With windows being impractical in this domical vault the only remaining way to illuminate the area of the crossing was to place windows in the transept lunettes, but above their barrel vaults. This required lower crossing arches. Accordingly, the span of the arches to the shallow transept vaults was reduced by 1.16 meters.

There remained the problem of the nave and sanctuary barrel vaults. Since the crossing vault would rise well above them Fray Francisco reduced the span of the nave and sanctuary crossing arches by 1.5 meters (to 11.7). By lowering their height he thereby created "proper" triumphal arches.

The solution to this involved structural problem resulted in a distinctive pier-buttress column design for the crossing positions (Fig. 3.56). Its irregular shaped base, a good meter high, is 1.37 wide on the nave side, projecting into the nave .75 centimeters. The transept side echoes the nave side but, to accommodate the even shorter radius of the transept arches, that pedestal projects another 58 centimeters.

Extending out from the nave wall are interiorized buttresses (1.37 by 3.7). These form chapels, six to a side, each 5.14 by 3.7. Interconnected by narrow passageways, they provided a private space for friars to say Mass. Clearly, basilican aisles were never intended.

It is evident that, from the outset, Fray Marín intended Santo Domingo to be closed with barrel, not ribbed, vaults. To that end he created the massive nave piers (2.8 by 0.90) and buttresses to bear the weight of the continuous nave vault. To counter its thrust he set the barrel vaults of the chapels at right angles thereto. By converting aisles into side chapels, and by narrowing their nave entrances, the architect visually created a single-nave church.

Analysis

The design sequence from rib- to barrel-vaulted nave churches would seem to be: Yanhuitlán, Coixtlahuaca, and finally Santo Domingo in Oaxaca. Dimensions are impressive—lengths, respectively, of 79, 63 and 78 meters. All are clearly by the same hand, works of an inspired architect.

In Santo Domingo Yanhuitlán Fray Francisco Marín reflects the style then popular in Spain of continuous-nave, transept-less churches with 1:5 ratios. Its most impressive feature is the tremendous volume of the virtually undemarcated nave. Ribbed vaults and classic entablatures reflect the uneasy Gothic-Renaissance marriage being experienced in sixteenth-century Spain.

At San Juan Bautista Coixtlahuaca Fray Francisco introduced interiorized buttresses, jutting out from the walls at 12-meter intervals.

FIGURE 3.55. Santo Domingo, view of nave looking toward sanctuary.

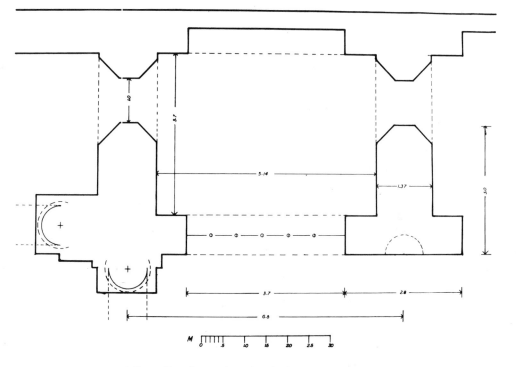

FIGURE 3.56. Santo Domingo, plan, detail of pier-buttress design at crossing.

The four rib-vaulted nave bays thereby became 12-meter squares with "appendages." These, however, are not interconnected; access is from the nave through arches with an 11.8 span. The Gothic-Renaissance spirit still lingers.

In Santo Domingo, Oaxaca, Fray Marín becomes a full-fledged Renaissance architect. Beneath the almost overwhelming impact of the glittering white and gold stucco (seventeenth century) covering all interior surfaces lies the evidence. Barrel vaults have replaced ribbed vaults. The apse is squared. The aisles become side chapels. The nave side of the latter is given a wide face reducing the entrance width into the chapels to 3.65 meters. The smaller nave arches and wider "piers" create the effect much more of a pierced wall than an arcade. Now the interior has been transformed into a broad single nave with defined bays, a large domed crossing, shallow transepts, and a squared sanctuary.

Vignola is universally acclaimed for his dynamically new design changing the three-aisled basilica into a single-nave church. Il Gesu, says Kostov, presents "a broad, barrel vaulted nave flanked by a series of subordinate chapels, a shallow transept with a dome over the crossing,"[31] a description which fits Santo Domingo equally well. Il Gesu was started in 1568. If Santo Domingo was started soon after Fray Francisco Marín's stay in Oaxaca from 1547 to 1548, then his design anticipates Vignola's by almost twenty years!

If this newly discovered architect, Fray Francisco Marín, had created these three churches in the Old World rather than the New, he would long ago have been ranked among the great architects of the Renaissance.

SUGGESTED READING

Kubler, George. *Mexican Architecture of the Sixteenth Century.* Greenwood Press, 1972. Originally published in 1948 by Yale University Press. 2 vols.

McAndrew, John. *The Open-Air Churches of Sixteenth-Century Mexico, Atrios, Posas, Open Chapels, and Other Studies.* Harvard University Press, 1965.

Mullen, Robert. *Dominican Architecture in Sixteenth-Century Oaxaca.* Arizona State University, Center for Latin American Studies, 1975.

———. *The Architecture and Sculpture of Oaxaca, 1530s–1980s.* Arizona State University, Center for Latin American Studies, 1995.

Peterson, Jeanette Favrot. *The Paradise Garden Murals of Malinalco: Utopia and Empire in Sixteenth-Century Mexico.* University of Texas Press, 1993.

Pierce, Donna. "The Mission: Evangelical Utopianism in the New World (1523–1600)," in *Mexico, Splendors of Thirty Centuries,* The Metropolitan Museum of Art.

Toussaint, Manuel. *Colonial Art in Mexico.* University of Texas Press, 1967, Chapter Five.

Weismann, Elizabeth Wilder. *Art and Time in Mexico.* Harper & Row, 1985; Icon paperback, 1995.

4

Cathedrals: Symbols of Authority

⊷─⊰≣◈≣⊱─⊷

D URING the Viceregency, Church and State shared power
and authority. The symbols for such were manifested in
architecture—the cathedral and the government building.
Yet everywhere throughout the colony the former outrivaled the latter. Even Mexico City's block-long National Palace, now three-story
but then a two-story structure, is overshadowed by the imposing size
of the adjacent Cathedral. In Spanish cities throughout Nueva España,
cathedrals proclaimed the ascendancy of the secular clergy. In the
cathedrals the bishops, as the representatives of the Pope, resided and
ruled their diocese. Cathedrals were meant to impress the new subjects of Spain as supreme examples of ultimate dominion. The Crown
lavished its best talent and tithes on their construction. These were the
works of architects from Spain, some of the foremost in the land.

In Nueva España during the sixteenth century, seven dioceses were
established that covered most of the central highlands and Yucatán.
The seats of these bishoprics were the new, strategically located, Spanish cities of México, Puebla, Morelia, Guadalajara, Oaxaca, San
Cristóbal de las Casas, and Mérida. Each first bishop built his cathedral. All but one of these structures were replaced or modified; only
Mérida's cathedral boasts its original 16-century fabric. Plans for the
"newer" cathedrals were often made during the sixteenth century,
but, in general, construction did not begin until the seventeenth.

During that century more cathedrals were built in Mexico than in Spain.

Cathedrals were created throughout the colonial epoch. Those early ones designed from the ground up as cathedrals look European and were often more "Spanish" than their counterparts at home, accurately reflecting the current Renaissance or Baroque styles as practiced in Spain. Later, during the eighteenth century, those parish churches transformed into cathedrals reflect a new, nonderivative style.

Cathedrals erected in the seventeenth century were predominantly basilican structures. Design was based upon proportions and the geometries of the circle, square, and equilateral triangle. The Renais-

FIGURE 4.1. Mérida: Cathedral, west front.

sance style determined sculptural treatment. The apostles or saints were depicted in quiet repose. Classical orders—Doric, Ionic, Corinthian—proclaimed the facade in a clearly articulated architectural framework. Sobriety, compartmentation, and ordered sequence, dominated the facade. The cathedrals of Mérida, Mexico City, and Guadalajara are examples.

Certain features characterize the early cathedrals of Nueva España. In most, the area between the towers describes a square. In the lower half, the facade and tower bases form a long horizontal rectangle (in contrast to the tall vertical rectangle of the pueblo church). The facade is divided into three parts. A large door occupies the central, larger zone, smaller doors the other two (echoing the nave and aisles of the interior). Facade and walls were constructed of smoothly cut and evenly layered stone. From the entrance the main altar seems far removed. The choir occupies most of the west end of the nave; choir stalls are masterpieces of wood carving. The cruciform plan is evident only in the interior. The crossing is covered with a dome. Museum-quality statues and oil paintings enrich altars in chapels flanking the side aisles, yet separated from them by wrought iron screens.[1] The glittering, polished, multicolored finish of the interior contrasts sharply with the monochrome of the exterior.

MÉRIDA (Yucatán)

The Diocese of Yucatán was established in 1562 and Mérida's present cathedral begun. Several architects were involved, the last being Juan Miguel de Agüera, engaged there from 1585 until the cathedral was completed in 1597. This structure stands intact. The north tower also belongs to the sixteenth century; the south tower was completed in 1710. Formal consecration did not occur until 1763.

The austere simplicity of Mérida's facade with its rough finish of layered stone makes it unlike any other cathedral in Mexico (Fig. 4.1). Its three doors are "lost" in the great unbroken mass of the west front with its slightly projecting tower bases. Renaissance pediments and finials frame the arched portals. The larger, central one carries paired Ionic columns framing Saints Peter and Paul. A 30-by-17-

FIGURE 4.2. Mérida: Cathedral, facade detail, royal escutcheon.

meter "triumphal arch" rises above the facade and occupies almost two-thirds of its width. Beneath the arch, mounted atop very tall engaged piers, is a large escutcheon surrounded with Plateresque floral designs (Fig. 4.2). An inscription identifies it as the coat of arms of Philip II and bears the date 1599.

The architect of Mérida's "hall church," with nave and aisles of approximately the same height, is unknown.[2] The cathedral's interior measures 66 by 31.5 meters. In plan the configuration of a cross within this rectangle is made clear by a distinctive vaulting pattern. Rectangular vaults, covered with a network of ribs, adorn four nave bays, two transept arms and two sanctuary bays. These eight units,

FIGURE 4.3. Mérida: Cathedral, view from rear toward crossing and sanctuary.

together with the squared crossing, form a cross. Nave bays are defined by huge, plain columns, two meters in diameter, with Tuscan capitals. Their vaults derive their distinctive shape from the differing diameters of the intersecting ribs forming coffers which become distended at the spring (Fig. 4.3). The pattern of the cross, so apparent in plan, is not so evident to the viewer. Since there are no clearstory windows, most of the light comes from windows in the drum supporting the crossing dome. The light is intense and fosters a sense of disorientation. The choir has always been located in the first bay at the west end of the nave. There are no side chapels.

The Cathedral of Mérida, facing west onto a lovely plaza dense with trees, is imposing, unique. Its west front complies with controlling geometries. A square (42 by 42 meters) can be inscribed around the base and towers. The base of the coat of arms is at the intersection of the diagonals. A circle can be inscribed from the facade base to the inside edge of the towers and to the top of the arch framing the coat of arms. An equilateral triangle has a base between the towers and its apex at the choir window sill.[3]

MEXICO CITY (Distrito Federal)

The cornerstone for the present Cathedral of Mexico was laid in 1573 based upon a plan by Claudio de Arciniega, a Spanish architect who had arrived in Mexico in 1558.[4] Construction proceeded slowly, with many changes.[5] Most of the cathedral was built in the seventeenth century. It was first consecrated in February, 1645, and rededicated in December 1667, upon completion of the vaulting. The facade, however, was still incomplete. Belfries, 61 meters high, were not finished until 1791. The cathedral was finally completed in the early 1800s by Manuel Tolsa, a Spanish architect and proponent of the then popular neoclassic style. To him can be credited the cupola with tall lantern, the cube with clock, and the statues in the facade center.

The lower rectangular portion of the cathedral (Fig. 4.4) reflects the severe Renaissance style introduced into Spain by Juan de Herrera in his formidable Escorial. Massive tower bases of precisely cut grey stone are pierced with square openings illuminating stairwells. The tower bases frame a slightly recessed facade composed of three verti-

FIGURE 4.4. Mexico City: Cathedral, south (main) front (Instituto de Investigaciones Estéticas, Universidad Nacional Autónoma de México).

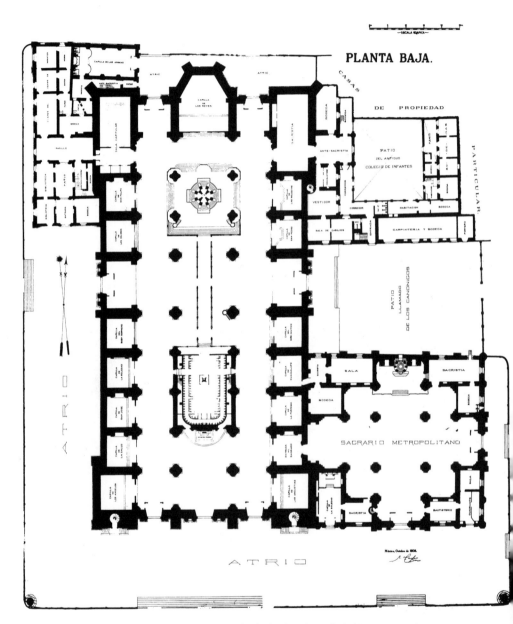

FIGURE 4.5. Mexico City: Cathedral, plan (*Vocabulario arquitectónico
ilustrado*, Secretaría del Patrimonio Nacional, México).

cal zones separated by powerful buttresses. The central portal is wider and higher than the other two. Each portal is framed by paired fluted columns with Doric capitals and entablature. In addition, the central one has figures of Saints Peter and Paul standing at repose in niches between the paired columns. The aesthetic of this lower part of the facade derives from the consistent precision of its proportions. Facade and towers conform to a square, tower height being that of base length. The clock above the crest sits precisely at the intersection of the diagonals.

Upon entering the cathedral (117 by 69 meters) from the central portal, one encounters a resplendent metal screen (dated to 1723) filling the space between the nave piers, completely blocking the view to the main altar.[6] On a sunlit day the interior is bathed in a soft golden glow as light enters clearstory windows through translucent slabs of onyx. The Doric/Tuscan order prevails in the rank of columns. Groined vaults close the five-bay nave; domical vaults, supported by engaged columns, the side aisles. Dimly lit chapels are attached to each bay and entered by passing through wrought iron screens closing each. Lateral walls and the screen between the nave columns define the choir which occupies the third and fourth nave bays as evidenced in the plan (Fig. 4.5). The rhythmic cadence of the five nave and aisle bays is interrupted by the crossing (15.5 by 15.5) and transept. Here the outline of the Latin cross is manifest. A magnificent octagonal dome set on a windowed drum crowns the crossing. The main altar area occupies the second of four bays extending beyond the crossing which then terminates in a polygonal apse. The latter is filled with a gilt retablo known as the *Altar de los Reyes*, completed in 1736.

An unusual feature of the Cathedral, known locally as the Metropolitan Cathedral, is that the intended east-west orientation was changed to north-south, with the facade facing south, to accommodate the large colonial structures already built on the Plaza Mayor. The massive cathedral is set upon unstable ground, much of it over the area of the Main Temple of the Aztec ceremonial center. Consequently, after four centuries there is a difference of more than two meters elevation between the north and south faces despite the foundations being regularly stabilized.

FIGURE 4.6. Guadalajara: Cathedral, west front.

GUADALAJARA (Jalisco)

A third example of a cathedral with a Renaissance facade is the one in Guadalajara. Although a diocese was approved in 1548, the cornerstone of the present cathedral was not laid until 1591; it was dedicated in 1618. The present towers are replacements of the originals which had collapsed in the 1818 earthquake. Bases are original. Towers and the huge bow across the facade were executed in 1853–1854, including the relief depicting the Assumption (Fig. 4.6).[7] Despite these additions, the quiet, sober, harmonious design of the facade's rectangle stands out. Its length is three times its height. A pleasing thrust-counterthrust effect is created by the solid vertical lines made by the six pilasters and the double horizontals of the cornice. Unlike any other cathedral front, the angled and wider-end pilasters make the tower bases appear slender (Fig. 4.7). The Doric and Corinthian

capitals on the portals are strictly Classic. The small sculptures of the
Virgin Mary, Saint Peter and Saint Paul in the central panel of the
second tier are emphasized by the discreet shadows of the circular
windows over the side portals. In placing the axes of the side portals
off-center towards the central portal the architect gave all three a
tight design. Guadalajara's facade by the architect, Martín Casillas,
active after 1585, is a gem among Mexico's Renaissance cathedral
facades.

Entering through one of the Renaissance portals, one is surprised
by a Gothic interior (Fig. 4.8). It appears similar to that of many
nineteenth-century neo-Gothic churches, but this interior was mod-
eled after those in Spain, where rib-vaulted interiors remained popular
well into the sixteenth century. The same architect, Casillas, also
designed the interior as a "hall church" with aisles the same height as
the nave, as in Mérida's cathedral. Vaults are high-pitched, upheld by

FIGURE 4.7. Guadalajara: Cathedral, west front, lower tier.

FIGURE 4.8. Guadalajara: "Gothic" interior,
view toward sanctuary.

slender piers with engaged fluted half columns crowned with Tuscan capitals. The shafts and capitals are white with gold trim.

Six rectangular bays, with neither crossing nor transept, make up the nave. Each is closed with a 12-part, 5-boss ribbed vault measuring 12 by 9 meters. Aisle bays are 9 by 9 squares with 8-part, single-boss vaults. A seventh bay is attached to the nave, taken up completely by a domed choir. The altar is placed in the sixth bay, the sanctuary floor raised ten steps. Because natural light enters the building only from the windows in the outer walls (and the choir dome) the interior is normally so dim that crystal chandeliers are lit for services.

By the mid-seventeenth century the livelier and lighter qualities of Spanish Baroque found fashion in cathedral facades, such as that in Puebla. A fine example of a late seventeenth–century facade is the cathedral in Oaxaca City.

PUEBLA (Puebla)

The Diocese of Puebla de los Angeles was established in 1531. The bishopric was located in Tlaxcala until 1543 when the bishop transferred his seat to Puebla. A plan for the cathedral, drawn up by the architects Francisco Becerra and Juan de Cigorondo, had been approved in 1575. Foundations were well along in 1580.[8] Major construction, however, was delayed until 1615. The original plan for a building with nave and aisles of the same height was changed in the 1620s by Luis Gómez de Transmonte to the standard basilican plan with nave higher than aisles—to provide better illumination of the nave. When the interior was completed in 1649, Puebla's cathedral was dedicated. Mosén Pedro García Ferrer from Valencia was the principal architect during the final years. During the Revolution (1910–1920) the cathedral was damaged; from 1926 to 1929 it was closed. In 1933, it was declared a National Monument. Major restorations were made during the 1980s.

Compared with Mexico City's cathedral, the cathedral in Puebla has a more unified, tighter design on the west front, the result of a concentrated building campaign (Fig. 4.9). The facade was completed during the 1660s (the square window in the crest carries the date 1664). The same elongated flat rectangle exists below the towers (north tower, 1678; south tower, 1731–1768), but the heaviness of Mexico's facade has been softened by placing three windows over the portals instead of relief panels. Verticals balance the horizontal by continuing the strong upward lines of the buttresses into the crest enclosed within a graceful curve. The lack of a persistent horizontal makes Puebla's facade less rooted to the ground. It terminates with a shining object "suspended" like a glittering jewel from the curves of the crest. It is the coat of arms of the Royal Crown.

The cathedral's facade follows the same square, diagonal, and equilateral triangle geometries as Mexico's, except for its towers, which extend well beyond the parameters of the square. The escutcheon of

FIGURE 4.9. Puebla: Cathedral, west front.

the Royal Crown sits precisely at the intersection of the diagonals. Puebla's tile-covered cupola has a lower profile; nonetheless, the tip of the cupola spire fits within the circle drawn within the square.[9]

In plan, the Cathedral of Puebla is almost identical to that in Mexico. It is, however, shorter because there are only four nave bays. Here the choir is adjacent to the crossing, occupying the third and fourth nave bays. The choir is an intact marvel of seventeenth-century artistry. The organ, with hundreds of pipes, is particularly striking. Wrought iron screens effectively "conceal" the side chapels, the fourth and fifth "aisles." Immediately above these chapels clear glass windows illuminate handsome domical aisle vaults adorned with mock coffers. Nave, transept and sanctuary have barrel vaults, groined in their lower half to accommodate lunettes with circular windows. Pendentives carry a circular dome over the crossing. The soft gray of towering composite piers, their shafts fluted from base to Tuscan capitals, complements the lustrous white (with gold trim) of the vaults.

In the nineteenth century the 82-by-51-meter interior was refashioned in a neoclassic mode, making it much brighter than the interior of Mexico's cathedral. The colonial retablo mayor was replaced by the huge neoclassic altar now gracing the raised sanctuary (which occupies the second of the three bays beyond the crossing). One of the few remaining colonial features in the Cathedral is the mural by Cristóbal de Villalpando covering the dome over the apse.

OAXACA (Oaxaca)

The Cathedral of Oaxaca boasts one of the finest late-seventeenth-century facades in Mexico. By the late seventeenth century the structure had undergone three building stages.[10] The cathedral sits on the north side of the main plaza with the south nave flanking the plaza and the facade, oriented to the west, facing its own small plaza.

The Cathedral was begun soon after the Diocese of Oaxaca was established in 1535. In 1544 the cathedral was described as having "columns made of one piece of stone, quite tall and thick."[11] The presence of these monolithic columns implies that the cathedral had three aisles or, more accurately, a nave and two side aisles (Fig. 4.10). This basilican structure with wooden ceilings and gabled, tiled roofs was changed completely in the 1670s with the decision to vault the

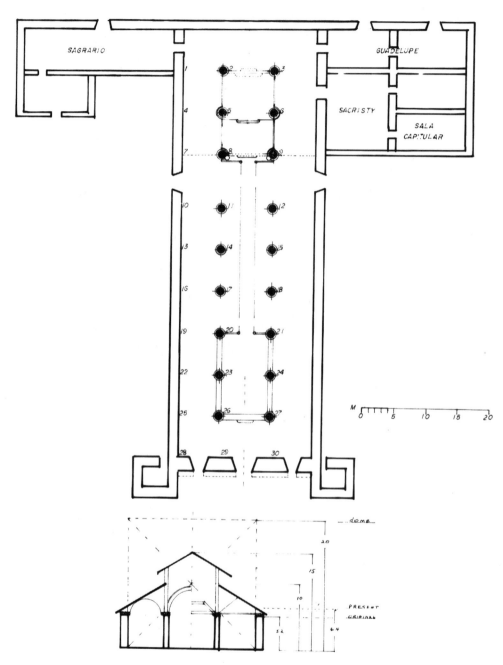

FIGURE 4.10. Oaxaca: Cathedral, plan (1535).

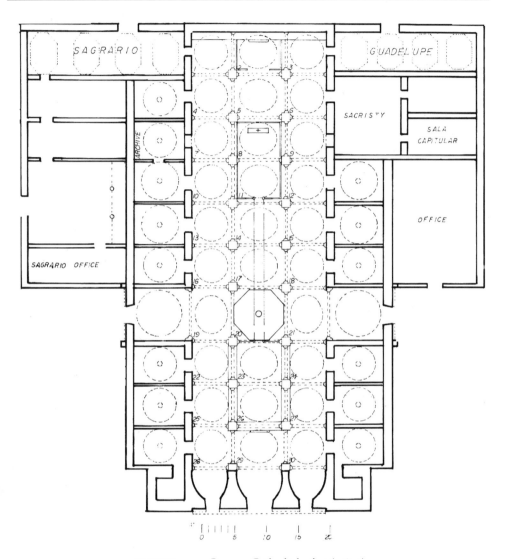

FIGURE 4.11. Oaxaca: Cathedral, plan (1694).

thirty-bay interior.[12] Maestro José González completed his commission in 1678. Fourteen side chapels (fourth and fifth aisles) were
added in 1682. The plan of Oaxaca's cathedral as it appeared in 1694
is that seen today (Fig. 4.11). Nave and aisles retain their sixteenth-
century dimensions of 66.5 by 21 meters. A nave bay still measures 8

FIGURE 4.12. Oaxaca: Cathedral,
view from crossing to choir.

by 6.5, an aisle bay 6 by 6. Since 1682 the cathedral has measured 66.5 by 39 meters.

Walls of the vaulted nave and aisles have lunettes, each with a window. North-south arches transversing the rectangular naves have their spring above the cornice, set above the lateral arches, creating a ballooning effect in the vault (Fig. 4.12). Transepts are virtual squares; their vaults are the same height as those of the nave. The crossing bears an octagonal dome on a drum.

Once the transformation from a timbered to a vaulted interior was completed, fashioning a new and "appropriate" facade would have taken priority. A superb design was expertly executed, most likely

FIGURE 4.13. Oaxaca: Cathedral facade, set forward of tower bases.

between 1685 and 1700.[13] Two broad, unadorned towers stoutly embrace the facade even though part of it extends beyond their plane (Fig. 4.13). Within the 35-meter west front, the facade measures 21 meters and is almost a square. Architectural features clearly delineate five vertical sections held firmly in place by three strong horizontal cornices marking the three tiers. These are of different heights, diminishing as they ascend, creating a subtle rhythm. There are the usual three entrances, but the side portals have been permanently closed. The facade exhibits the struggle between antipodes: clear, architectural line (Renaissance) and diffuse, overwhelming sculpture (Baroque). Unique to Oaxaca's facade is its pale green stone that, at certain times of the day, literally glows.

Saints Peter and Paul quietly guard the main entrance. Four more statues, in a contemplative mood, occupy niches in the second and third tiers. Among the six relief panels the one in the center of the second tier dominates. This is an action scene. Faces of the gesticulating apostles are filled with emotions as Mary's glorified body is borne aloft by angels into Heaven. (Fig. 4.14). This moment of her Assumption is set within a heavy, elaborately carved frame with ponderous, stepped corners. (These "broken" corners are first seen in a much more discreet rendition in the relief panels of Mexico's Cathedral.) This facade is among the masterpieces of cathedral sculpture created in the last quarter of the seventeenth century in Nueva España.

What happened to the sixteenth-century facade? In that era facades were recessed well behind the front plane of the towers. At Oaxaca the facade juts out beyond that plane. This fact and the unusual thickness of the west wall suggest that the present facade was erected directly over the original. There is a precedent for this in Oaxaca: Yanhuitlán's facade covers another.

With the exploitation of the mineral wealth in the vast area north of Mexico City, population expanded rapidly, sustaining a growth rate which, by the eighteenth century, was sufficient to warrant new bishoprics. Dioceses were created and bishops took up residence in Zacatecas, Chihuahua, Durango, Monterrey, and Saltillo. Here cathedrals were not built from the ground up. Parish churches were elevated to the rank of cathedral. In Michoacán, however, a cathedral,

FIGURE 4.14. Oaxaca: Cathedral facade, central relief, Mary's Assumption.

designed as such, arose in the late seventeenth century but with a facade created in the eighteenth century.

MORELIA (Michoacán)

Although the Diocese of Michoacán was established in 1536, the present cathedral, designed by Vicente Barroso de la Escayola, was begun in 1660 and dedicated in 1705 (Fig. 4.15). José de Medina designed the facade. It was completed by 1711, the date inscribed in the crest. Belfries, 62 meters tall, were erected in 1744. In the late nineteenth century the interior was extensively renovated in the neoclassic style.

The north-facing main entrance (Fig. 4.16) displays key eighteenth-century features—compressed center panel; heavy vertical accent; broken horizontals; elements projecting into the next tier;

FIGURE 4.15. Morelia: Cathedral, view from northeast.

FIGURE 4.16. Morelia: Cathedral, facade.

segmented crest line; oval windows; gesticulating figures; contrasting dark and light stones. Its dynamism makes any seventeenth-century cathedral seem somnolent. The lively nature of Morelia's facade seems incongruent with the very large, unadorned tower bases. Ponderous, extending 13 meters to each side of the facade, they command silence. By contrast the belfries are richly ornamented. They and the facade shout Hosanna! The light-colored relief panels with their gesticulating figures give emphasis to the sense of movement, to an event, as in the central relief, *The Transfiguration of Christ* (Fig. 4.17). The relief on the left is the *Adoration of the Shepherds;* that on the right the *Adoration of the Three Kings.* Thematic selections concentrate on the life of Christ rather than the attributes of the Mother of God.

The interior is 70 by 28 meters (Fig. 4.18). From the entrance, four rectangular bays (11 by 8.5) of considerable height lead to the

FIGURE 4.17. Morelia: Cathedral, facade, central relief, *Transfiguration of Christ.*

11-by-11 crossing. Illumination comes through elliptical windows inserted in lunette walls at the vault spring. A circular dome with eight windows in the drum is supported by pendentives. Transept arms, the same size as a nave bay, are more a continuation of the side aisles (there are no side chapels) than projections from the crossing. Only on the exterior are they clearly visible as such, first by their portals, then by their height, notably greater than the aisle walls. Beyond

FIGURE 4.18. Morelia: Cathedral, view from rear toward sanctuary.

the crossing, the aisles extend another three bays, the nave another four. The main altar is in the second bay while a large choir is located in the third and fourth. With the choir at the end opposite the main entrance, the interior of the Cathedral of Morelia seems spacious and gracious.

ZACATECAS (Zacatecas)

Since its founding in 1548, Zacatecas has been a flourishing silver-mining community. The Cathedral sits directly on the narrow main street, as did two previous churches (Fig. 4.19). Begun in 1729 as a parish church, its three-aisle design is attributed to the architect, Domingo Ximénez Hernández. Vaults were in place by 1741, and by 1745 the west front and its facade were completed. Although dedicated in 1752, the side portals were not completed until 1775–1777. The south tower was added only in 1782, the north not until 1904. This elegant parish church was elevated to the rank of cathedral in 1862, three years after the Diocese of Zacatecas was created.

Zacatecas was one of five parish churches erected in the northern part of Mexico during the eighteenth century that boasted three aisles.[14] Interior dimensions are 58.5 by 33.5 meters (Fig. 4.20). An elevated choir occupies the first nave bay as is usual in parish churches, then follow three more nave bays, the crossing, and the sanctuary.[15] Illumination was dim until a new octagonal dome with larger windows was constructed in 1846. During the nineteenth century virtually all traces of eighteenth-century decor were replaced by neoclassic embellishment. Work done between 1964 and 1965 restored the interior closer to its original state.

The facade is like a gigantic retablo (Fig. 4.21). Tensions arise between the solid architecture of the tower bases and the profuse decor of the facade. Its single portal belies its three-aisled interior. Of the facade's three tiers, the first two carry six large columns, the third only four, all richly and deeply carved. A large circular choir window, framed with sprightly angels in high relief, occupies the entire center panel above the portal. Thirteen facade niches contain Christ (top, center) and the twelve apostles. Other iconography refers to the Immaculate Conception, the Trinity, and the Eucharist, symbolized by a profusion of grapes and angels with musical instruments. Bulky

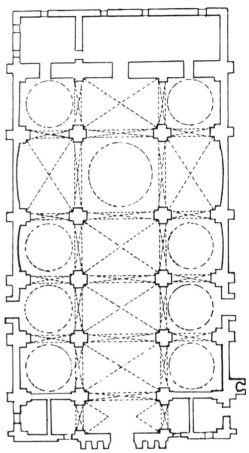

FIGURE 4.19. Zacatecas: Cathedral, street view from south.

FIGURE 4.20. Zacatecas: Cathedral, plan (*La arquitectura de la plata*,
Clara Bargellini, Instituto de Investigaciones Estéticas, Universidad Nacional
Autónoma de México, México).

columns framing the statues display deeply undercut (up to three
inches) high relief. The statues don't catch the eye—the decoration,
almost smothering them, does.

The crest is a marvel of intricate sculpture. Deeply cut floral
arrangements with individual patterns uniquely outlined by drilled
holes constitute the frame which then flows continuously along the

outer edges of the third-tier panoply. Not an inch of the enclosure is left void. In the center of the crest a bearded Christ is Ruler of the Universe. Not many are initially apt to see four adoring angels to each side, joyously singing His praises to the accompaniment of musical instruments. It seems unlikely that whoever carved this lively plani-form relief also carved the solemn figures in the niches. These latter reflect the expertise of an academically trained sculptor. The crest reliefs echo local sensibilities. The unified design, thematic content, and exuberant sculpture make Zacatecas' facade unique in colonial Mexico both as parish church and as cathedral.

SALTILLO (Coahuila)

The small Spanish settlement of Saltillo was founded in 1577. It soon became an agricultural and commercial center and eventually the capital of the state.[16] Because of population growth the pastor decided, in 1745, to build a larger parish church with a single nave (57 by 12 meters). In 1795 it was dedicated to Santiago (Saint James, Apostle). The Diocese of Saltillo was not established until 1891, at which time the church of Santiago was elevated to the rank of cathe-dral. Two years later the neoclassic belfry was erected. In 1923 the original main altar was replaced with the present neoclassic piece. Sev-eral colonial altars and paintings grace the interior, still largely in its original condition.

The cathedral faces west onto a large plaza. One first sees the bel-fry, so immense its base had to be enlarged (Fig. 4.22). This three-story nineteenth-century addition dominates, almost overpowers, the eighteenth-century facade, completed by 1785. While the five vertical sections are a familiar feature, possibly inspired by Zacatecas, styles in the tiers differ. In the first tier garlanded, solomonic columns reflect Mexico's academic version of early eighteenth-century Baroque. In the second tier, the "squared" estípite columns feature Mexico's own late-eighteenth-century contribution to the arts. The third tier with its niche and shell is a diminutive version of the first tier.[17] The upward rush of the six verticals is stopped by a series of counterswirls anchored in place by compact floral finials. The brilliant design of Saltillo's facade is one that could have been created only in the second half of the eighteenth century.

FIGURE 4.21. Zacatecas: Cathedral, facade, three tiers and crest.

FIGURE 4.22 Saltillo: Cathedral, west front.

By the end of the eighteenth century tastes had changed. Then, and for most of the nineteenth century, neoclassic sedateness prevailed as exemplified in the Cathedral of Puebla's renovated interior. A long period of neglect of Mexico's cathedrals followed the Revolution of 1910. Today the eighteen cathedrals erected during the Viceregency are considered national treasures. Preservation and restoration are now key objectives.

SUGGESTED READING

Bargellini, Clara. *La arquitectura de la plata: Iglesias monumentales del centro-norte de México.* UNAM, Instituto de Investigaciones Estéticas, 1991, Chapter Four and pp. 259–292.

Catedrales de México. Mexico City, 1993.

Toussaint, Manuel. *Colonial Art in Mexico.* University of Texas Press, 1967, pp. 109–115.

———. *La Catedral de México, México.* Editorial Porrua, 1973.

Weismann, Elizabeth. *Art and Time in Mexico.* Harper & Row, 1985; Icon edition, 1995, pp. 151–167.

5

Transitional Phase:
From the
Static to the Dynamic

(Mid-Seventeenth to Mid-Eighteenth Century)

⟶ ⟼ ✦ ⟻ ⟵

MANUEL TOUSSAINT was one of the first scholars to identify Mexico's architecture, sculpture, and painting of the 100-year period from the mid-seventeenth to the mid-eighteenth centuries as "Baroque." He does so, however, almost apologetically, writing, "One thing is certain: that the Baroque style in Mexico evolves according to its own particular nature. Undoubtedly it derives from European Baroque, but its development is so special, so unique, that it would be foolish to try to explain it by reference to European theories. The relationship is rather one of similarity in mood. . ."[1] He compounds the dilemma by later creating three categories of Baroque architecture: ". . . it began by being 'sober'; then, as the ornament preponderated, it became 'rich'; and finally toward the end of the seventeenth century it reached such a stage of luxuriance in some places that it can only be termed 'exuberant.'"[2] Thereafter "Mexican Baroque" became part of the lexicon, in spite of its imprecision.

The art historian Elizabeth Wilder Weismann handled the problem with insight and grace. She wrote:

"There is really no point in measuring New World architecture against Baroque in Rome, to discover that it lacks spatial invention. It is even a waste of time to argue whether there is a 'Mexican Baroque' or merely 'Baroque in Mexico,' or not even that . . . Baroque style arrived from Europe not only once, but in a succession of catalytic imports . . . Thus certain elements can be traced to cathedral Baroque—like domes which followed after Pedro García Ferrer built the first one (1640) on the Cathedral of Puebla . . . The next wave, which was felt around mid-seventeenth century, continues on into the 1730s, or even much later, here and there. One can generalize about this Baroque . . . (but) the buildings and altarpieces refuse to fall into perfect classifications."[3]

Octavio Paz, one of Mexico's greatest writers, delved into this discussion. In his introduction to *Mexico: Splendors of Thirty Centuries*, he wrote, "*Baroque* is a word whose origins and meaning is incessantly and eternally debated . . . The Baroque is solid and complete; at the same time it is fluid and fleeting. It congeals into a form that an instant later dissolves into a cloud . . . The Baroque of New Spain began as a branch of the Spanish tree. As it took root and grew in our soil, it was transformed into a different tree."[4]

Against this background of various and broad interpretations of "Mexican Baroque" this author prefers the more precise classification of defined spans of time, much like "quattrocento" defines the 1400s of Renaissance Italy. Then too, there is the differing architecture of city and pueblo. If "Baroque" can be applied to certain buildings in the cities of Mexico, it is impossible to apply the term to pueblo architecture of this period. The traits of a professional architect practicing in the city are readily distinguished. In the pueblo, personalities are discernible but the individual remains cloaked in anonymity. Names appear in parish records under baptisms, marriages, or burials, but master builders and artisans are seldom identified in local records. To be known by one's contemporaries was sufficient.

The difference between city sculpture and pueblo sculpture is even more distinctive. That in the city is academically "correct," executed according to the professional precepts of the time. That in the pueblo is essentially popular art. What these artists without formal training created defies classification. Pueblo sculpture is vibrantly individual, distinctive, and incomparable. It can indeed be "exuberant," at times seemingly out of control. The local priest, probably born and raised in a pueblo, would have been consulted about the iconography. Although he would have been trained in a seminary the priest's value system would have been more Indian than European. Hence, while the iconography derives from Christian Europe, the interpretation is often indigenous, even echoing ancient traditions. These works are best approached with non-Western eyes.

CITIES

MEXICO CITY (Distrito Federal)

To best understand the transition to the new style called Baroque, it is necessary to return to Mexico's cathedral. In Chapter 4, the cathedral's lower tier and its Renaissance characteristics were discussed. Completion of the upper tier between 1672 and 1689 set a "new" stylistic pace for the country as the Spanish Baroque made its debut in Nueva España. The large relief of Mary's Assumption in the second tier is eye-catching (Fig. 5.1). Even the relief's frame is no longer a simple square; jutting, squared corners give the impression that the Assumption is "hung" as if it were a painting. In this tier columns shafts are fluted their entire length rather than with a zigzag pattern in the lower third. Broken cornices relax the otherwise rigid horizontal line and a segmented arch lightens the third tier. The mass of the embracing buttresses is relieved by their shortened height topped with curving scrolls. Static-dynamic tensions epitomize late-seventeenth- and early-eighteenth-century facades most everywhere in Mexico.

Among the many devotional sites in Mexico none attracts more pilgrims than the Santuario de La Virgen de Guadalupe in the Villa de Guadalupe on the outskirts of Mexico City. Throngs converge daily, mostly by bus, but many walk hundreds of miles. The Virgin of Guadalupe is the heart of Mexico. In the struggle for independence she was *the* symbol around which the colony's forces coalesced. Her image remains as evocative today as the tricolor national flag.

Juan Diego, a native of the pueblo of Tepeyac, was a young man when, on a hill near his village, he saw an apparition—the figure of a

FIGURE 5.1. Mexico City: Cathedral, central relief,
Mary's Assumption (Instituto de Investigaciones Estéticas,
Universidad Nacional Autónoma de México, México).

FIGURE 5.2. Mexico City: Villa de Guadalupe, basilica, general view.

richly clothed woman. The woman asked Juan to seek out the Bishop (of nearby Mexico) and ask him to have a shrine built at that spot in her honor. Naturally, Bishop Zumárraga was skeptical. The lady appeared to Juan several times more, finally asking him to carry to the Bishop some flowers growing (in winter) on the hilltop. Doing as she requested, Juan put the flowers in his *tilma* (a cloak knotted at the shoulder) and hastened to Mexico. Granted an audience with the

Bishop, Juan Diego opened his cloak only to find the flowers replaced by an image of the lady "painted" on the tilma. The Bishop was convinced. The image became known as Our Lady of Guadalupe.[5] Rome has since proclaimed her Patroness of the Americas. By 1533 a small chapel had been built atop the hill near Tepeyac and Juan stood guard over his tilma until his death in 1548.

The last colonial shrine to Our Lady of Guadalupe was built between 1695 and 1709. The original plan by Pedro de Arrieta, a Latin cross with nave, two aisles, and internal transepts, was soon modified. Lateral arms, each 12.5 meters, reached out from the crossing, to make it a central-plan church. There are fourteen vaulted bays plus the dome over the crossing. The exterior dimensions remained unchanged at 54.5 by 38 meters.

All four corners of this colonial church have protruding octagonal tower bases crowned with two-tiered belfries over which soars a 40-meter-high dome (Fig. 5.2). The wide rectangular south wall with three portals opening onto an immense plaza is properly academic with its Classic Orders, paired columns, and clearly regulated zones. Yet this wall is no longer strictly planar. Belfries and the extra-wide central portal protrude to create a soft undulation. This sense of motion is enhanced by the markedly different heights of the first and second tiers. Lastly, the central relief provides a dynamic portrayal of one of Our Lady's apparitions to Juan Diego.

Over the years the structure has gradually subsided since its foundations lie on a lakebed. Dangerously out of plumb, the church is now closed. The new adjacent Basilica, designed by Pedro Ramírez Vásquez, was completed in the 1970s. Thousands gather under its tentlike concrete roof to have at long last an unobstructed view of La Virgen de Guadalupe.

San José el Real, known as "La Profesa" because of its Jesuit origin, was constructed between 1714 and 1720. Here Pedro de Arrieta, "the most famous architect of the period,"[6] mastered the new style. The interior is monumental, basilica in plan, with a great crossing and luminous cupola. The facade, however, presents only a single portal. The standard organization into three vertical zones and three horizontal tiers remains (Fig. 5.3). Yet because the first tier is a virtual square, higher spandrels result. This greater height makes the space between the paired columns, with their free-style Corinthian capitals, relatively narrow; the statues seem to be squeezed into their niches. The rectangular second tier permits the center relief with its "hanger" corners to be displayed prominently. In this tier not only the lower third of the columns but their pedestals as well are covered with deeply carved patterns. The third tier (not visible) has a huge octagonal óculo flanked with small free-standing statues. Diminutive and delicate scrolls provide a hint of a frame, giving this upper tier a relatively weightless appearance. The architect had freed himself from the rigidity of the Renaissance.

The Colegio de San Ignacio has always been called Las Vizcaínas because it was endowed by three Basque miners. Erected between 1734 and 1757 as a hospice and school for poor Spanish girls and widows, it still serves that purpose.[7] Four main patios, connected by passages and arcades, form the basic plan of the block-size building (Fig. 5.4). The more significant parts are: main entrance (2); main patio (12); chapel (15, 16); baths (27); garden (40); and classrooms (9, 28, 29, 31, 36, 37, 39). A monumental staircase (30) leads to the second floor.

In the extensive 128-meter street front, there are only two entrances, one leading to the chapel (Fig. 5.5). Its wall is made of tezontle, a native porous volcanic stone whose color varies from burgundy to rosy tan. Its majestic rhythmic cadence derives from beautifully proportioned rectangular bays, each defined by ground-to-roof gray *chiluca* limestone pilasters topped with finials. Each tezontle bay is pierced by rectangular and octagonal windows in stone "dog ear" frames. The overall impact is one of precision, quiet tension and authority. It is an imposing statement by an architect confidently handling a long stretch of masonry with restrained vigor.

The entrance to the chapel, reputedly designed by Lorenzo Rodríguez in 1786, is in a more dynamic style. The portal arch, emphasized by a lobed frame, rises into the entablature, where its curve is repeated fortissimo in the cornice. In the center of three niches stands the patron, Saint Ignatius, mirrored by the original octagonal window. This is one of the most beautiful and original of viceregal civic buildings.

FIGURE 5.3. Mexico City: "La Profesa," facade.

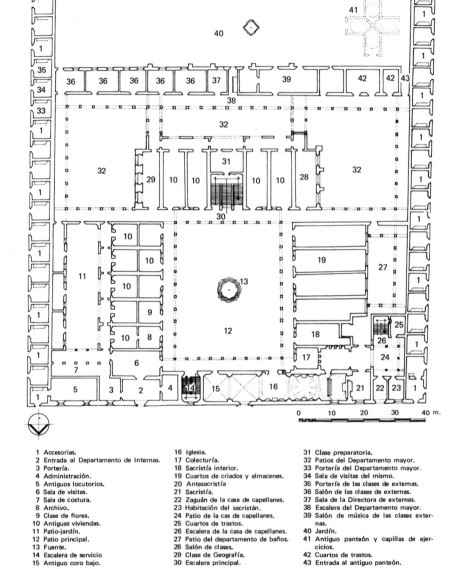

1 Accesorias.
2 Entrada al Departamento de Internas.
3 Portería.
4 Administración.
5 Antiguos locutorios.
6 Sala de visitas.
7 Sala de costura.
8 Archivo.
9 Clase de flores.
10 Antiguas viviendas.
11 Patio-jardín.
12 Patio principal.
13 Fuente.
14 Escalera de servicio
15 Antiguo coro bajo.

16 Iglesia.
17 Colecturía.
18 Sacristía interior.
19 Cuartos de criados y almacenes.
20 Antesacristía
21 Sacristía.
22 Zaguán de la casa de capellanes.
23 Habitación del sacristán.
24 Patio de la cas de capellanes.
25 Cuartos de trastos.
26 Escalera de la casa de capellanes.
27 Patio del departamento de baños.
28 Salón de clases.
29 Clase de Geografía.
30 Escalera principal.

31 Clase preparatoria.
32 Patios del Departamento mayor.
33 Portería del Departamento mayor.
34 Sala de visitas del mismo.
35 Portería de las clases de externas.
36 Salón de las clases de externas.
37 Sala de la Directora de externas.
38 Escalera del Departamento mayor.
39 Salón de música de las clases externas.
40 Jardín.
41 Antiguo panteón y capillas de ejercicios.
42 Cuartos de trastos.
43 Entrada al antiguo panteón.

FIGURE 5.4. Mexico City: Colegio "Las Vizcaínas," plan (*Vocabulario arquitectónico ilustrado*, Secretaría del Patrimonio Nacional, México).

FIGURE 5.5. Colegio "Las Vizcaínas," street view, entrance to chapel.

OAXACA (Oaxaca)

La Soledad in Oaxaca expresses that city's taste for the "new" style. A license to build a "new church" was granted on 3 January 1682; consecration took place on 6 September 1690. On that day the object of devotion, the "miraculous" statue of La Soledad (Mary, Mother of Sorrows) was transferred to its sumptuous new church.[8] On 18 January 1909, La Soledad was declared Patroness of the State of Oaxaca.

Directly behind the sanctuary, a small room, the *camarín*, is reserved exclusively for the statue of La Soledad. She is always regally attired according to the religious season, and her precious jewels and costly robes are stored here. The camarín contains an elevated niche, recessed in the wall behind the main altar, accessible by stairs. That part of the niche facing into the church is encased in glass, offering both protection and visibility as La Soledad is displayed to ever-present devotees.

In plan and proportions La Soledad church, though larger, does not vary radically from earlier parish churches in the city.[9] The interior dimensions of its cruciform plan are 54.5 by 13 meters (Fig. 5.6). The 13-by-13 crossing is closed with an octagonal drum and dome. A neoclassic altar is placed within the squared apse, dominated by the brightly illuminated, beautifully robed, and brilliantly jeweled statue of La Soledad. The nave consists of three bays and choir, each 8.3 by 13 meters. Domical vaults, with lanterns and lunette windows, form the closing. Transepts, also 8.3 by 13, are vaulted the same as the nave, with windows in all three walls.

The artistic glory of La Soledad is its 24-by-16-meter facade (Fig. 5.7). Facing east, it resembles a gigantic folding screen protruding three meters from the tower bases. Engaged columns unequivocally frame twenty-one divisions set in three horizontal tiers and seven vertical sections. The widest section is the recessed center with portal, relief, and choir window. This center section is surmounted with a

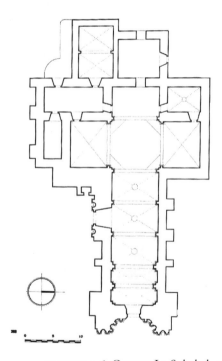

FIGURE 5.6. Oaxaca: La Soledad, plan.

FIGURE 5.7. La Soledad, facade (facing east).

FIGURE 5.8. La Soledad, facade, central relief, Mary at foot of Cross.

FIGURE 5.9. La Soledad, crest, relief of Immaculate Conception.

tall, rectangular crest depicting the Immaculate Conception in high relief. Ten niches contain life-size statues, all in repose. Smaller-scale reliefs, with themes from Mary's life, fill six panels. The narrowest sections are on each side of the center, partially angled. Next are wider sections, set at 45 degrees. The outermost sections are parallel to the center section. Following the precepts of the Classic Orders, the columns in the first tier have Doric capitals, the second, Ionic, and the third, Corinthian. To accommodate the height of the door, columns in the first tier are set upon pedestals. The horizontal demarcation of each tier by a heavy entablature and projecting cornice is as strong as the vertical columnar demarcation of sections. At the base of the door's arch, the date 1689 is inscribed.

La Soledad eloquently showcases the "controlled dynamic" style of sculpture preferred in Oaxaca toward the end of the seventeenth century. It features elegant yet restrained, joyous yet sober, eloquent figures within sturdy frames. Archangels, martyrs, virgins, apostles, and doctors of the Church confront the beholder in very lifelike, sometimes emotional, poses. A large magnificent relief above the door depicts the kneeling Mary at the foot of the cross (Fig. 5.8). So strong is her gesture and so poignant her expression that the viewer shares her sorrows. Later, one becomes aware of how oversized her figure is relative to the cross, and how deeply carved the stone frame is with its exaggerated corners.

The facade of the Cathedral and La Soledad are contemporaries, sharing many similarities. The free-standing figures have the same relaxed "Donatello-like" pose. The "dog-ear" frames of the central panels in both facades are virtual replicas. The Mary of the Assumption relief of the Cathedral (see Fig. 5.1) and the Mary of the Immaculate Conception of La Soledad in the crest are twins (Fig. 5.9). The church of San Agustín, whose facade was completed in 1698, displays similar characteristics.

The outpouring of devotion on La Soledad's feast day, the eighteenth of December, must be witnessed to be understood. Starting on the eve of the day itself, people from all parts of Oaxaca converge. By dusk the atrio and surrounding area are dense with worshippers, resonant with the soft sound of voices speaking many tongues. (Over twenty languages are still spoken in the State of Oaxaca.) People file slowly in and out of the church like an inexorable flow of lava. Inside they pay their fidelity to La Soledad, patiently waiting to glimpse the jeweled figure with the sad, delicate face. About midnight, the statue is removed from the camarín and carried through the church and into the atrio. The sense of joy is almost palpable as hosannas reach toward the sky. All through the night bands play, groups dance, the devout sing hymns, fireworks explode. A pontifical Mass is celebrated at noon, and La Soledad is once again proclaimed Patroness and Queen of the peoples of Oaxaca. She has remained the "heart" of Oaxaca through four centuries.

PUEBLA (Puebla)

Toussaint writes that a group of plasterworkers grew up in Puebla in mid-seventeenth century and developed to perfection the art of relief in stucco. They created a style that "seems to develop through caprice and fantasy."[10] It is often seen as "straps" woven over and under, covering every surface that is left. Toussaint believes the style reached its

FIGURE 5.10. Puebla: Santo Domingo, Rosary Chapel, view into dome.

FIGURE 5.11. Puebla: Santo Domingo, detail from arm of chapel.

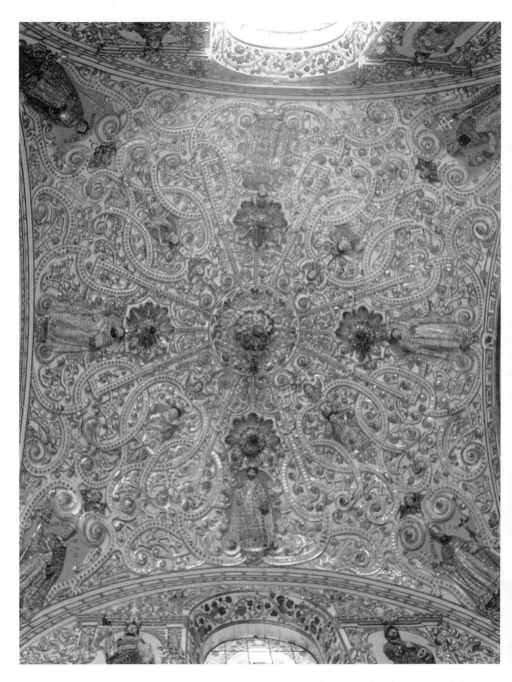

FIGURE 5.12. Oaxaca: Santo Domingo, crossing vault, stucco/gold "strap work."

climax in the Capilla del Rosario, an annex to the church of Santo Domingo in Puebla, and was moved to say:

> . . . The year 1690 is given by the historians as the terminal date of this monument; it should be read as the date of a miracle in our colonial architecture. This Rosary chapel is the climax of a type of church which represents the Mexican mood of that time in an extraordinary way. They say it was not built by anyone of wealth and power, but from the offerings of the pearl divers to the Virgin of the Rosary, their patron saint. . . . Here for the first time in the history of our country can we see the life of the nation embodied in unique form in a plastic creation.[11]

Upon entering the grottolike chapel, one is filled with awe.[12] Surfaces sparkle in gold and white. The eye seeks a place to rest, but the intertwining patterns are so intricate the eye is immediately drawn to another spot. Finally, the shape of the space enters one's consciousness. The dominating feature is the altar with a canopy enshrining a statue of the Virgin at the center of the chapel. Above rises a luminescent dome (Fig. 5.10), giving special luster to the gilded stucco work. Surrounding this domed space are three identical shallow arms and a fourth which links the chapel to the church. These arms are filled with sculpted foliage, animals, children, saints, and angels. Dancing light amidst these splendors lifts the spirit (Fig. 5.11).

Decorating the interior of churches with swirling stucco trimmed with gold had become popular by the mid-seventeenth century. In this decorative style architectural features are obscured by surface decor. Walls and vaults become "dematerialized." A well-known example is Santo Domingo in Oaxaca, whose interior stucco work was completed during the 1660s.[13] The eye is bedazzled by the intricacy of the design exemplified in the vaulted crossing where saints, cast in high relief, are framed in intricate "strap work" (Fig. 5.12).

CONVENTS

In the sixteenth century convents—religious institutions for women—existed in all cities of Mexico. Women of social standing during colonial times had only two choices: marriage or the religious life. The taking of vows was itself like a wedding ceremony, as seen in many colonial portraits of young nuns. Life at most convents entailed strict observance of rules, and minimal contact with the outside world.

Other convents were more residential, and women of wealth were permitted to have maids. Even a married woman could stay there when her husband was away for an extended time.

The architectural requirements of these cloistered institutions resulted in unique solutions. Living quarters were arranged around arcaded patios with access to individual rooms in a design much like that of a colegio. The conventual church, however, had to be accessible to the public as well as to the nuns, who had to remain cloistered. The church was therefore located so it flanked the street, offering two public entrances on that side. What was normally the facade was solid except for windows placed high in the wall. The lengthy interior was usually barrel vaulted.

A special portion of the nave, as much as one-third, opposite the sanctuary, was reserved for the nuns. The rest was open to the public. The area for the nuns, known in Spanish as the *coro* (not to be translated as "choir"), had two levels. Both levels are divided from the open nave by a formidable, often spectacular, metal screen (*reja*) reaching from floor to ceiling. During Mass, the nuns could see the priest in the sanctuary and the people in the nave, but they themselves could not be seen. Communion was distributed to the nuns through a small grille window in the screen. Once professed, a nun never left her convent, not even at death.

Only a few of the many colonial convents in Mexico still function as religious institutions. Once Mexico City had seventeen convents, Puebla eleven, Oaxaca several. Many have been transformed into schools and cultural centers. The former convent of Santa Catalina in Oaxaca is today the first-class El Presidente Hotel—an excellent example of adaptive reuse.

GUADALAJARA (Jalisco)

The former Augustinian convent of Santa Mónica is one of Guadalajara's sculptural jewels. Dating from the early part of the eighteenth century, most of the residential area was demolished at the end of the nineteenth century, but the church remains. The nave wall which flanks the street and has two entrances identifies it as having been a convent church (Fig. 5.13).

Every inch of these "public" portals, which probably were executed after the mid-eighteenth century, is filled with a variety of pat-

FIGURE 5.13. Guadalajara:
Santa Mónica, convent, with
two entrances on street side.

FIGURE 5.14. Santa Mónica,
portal, detail.

terns in high relief. Both are two-tiered, the upper separated from the lower by a wide band. The width of this band equals the height of the ground-level pedestals. By this device the length of the columns in both tiers remains the same. In the lower tier vines, dense with grapes, spiral around paired solomonic columns in a subtle mirror image design (Fig. 5.14). Between the columns, vertical panels are covered with a floral pattern in lower relief. The wide band separating the two tiers is filled with the two-headed (Hapsburg) eagle and angels. Rigorous architectural framework contrasts with vigorous sculptural treatment.

MORELIA (Michoacán)

The convent of Santa Catarina was constructed between 1729 and 1737. From afar twin polygonal crests in the nave wall proclaim this to be a convent (Fig. 5.15). The first tier of the twin portals is serenely classic, its fluted columns with Corinthian capitals standing upon plain socles. The second tier is enlivened by four small hooded but empty niches and a heavy molding around the top and sides of

FIGURE 5.15. Morelia: Santa Catarina, entrances into convent church.

FIGURE 5.16. Santa Catarina, view from coro (nuns' area) toward sanctuary.

the square window. The lines of this tier's four columns are carried into the third tier, linking the two. A pedimented niche is the central theme of this third tier on both portals, which lead into that part of the church used by the public. A dome, set on a drum, allows light to flood both the sanctuary and that part of the nave used by the public. From the relative dimness at the rear of the nave, the cloistered nuns looked through the metal grille of the coro into the illuminated church and sanctuary (Fig. 5.16). The retablo and altar where Mass is said are clearly visible. A similar reja shuts off the upper coro from the church.

HACIENDAS

The term "hacienda" has several applications, but it usually describes a large estate, covering thousands of acres, on which agricultural products or cattle were raised. In such an hacienda, living and work quarters were extensive, much like a plantation, except the hacienda complex was enclosed. Perimeter walls could extend over a thousand feet. The main entrance invariably had an impressive arched portal. This led to a large patio surrounded by arcades and rooms, usually single story. Two sides were living quarters for the owner's family; the third contained workrooms and store rooms. Often a chapel was located close to, or adjoining, the living areas. Although haciendas played a dominant role in the history of Mexico, their architecture was seldom significant except for that of the *hacienda de beneficio*, where minerals were processed after extraction.

SAN MIGUEL REGLA (Hidalgo)

Twenty miles north of the city of Pachuca, the capital of Hidalgo, lies this magnificent former hacienda for metal refining.[14] It was built by Pedro Romero de Terreros, the first Count of Regla, around the middle of the eighteenth century. The process for obtaining silver at the Hacienda de San Miguel Regla required large settling tanks. Ore, stone and chemicals were spread on the floor of these circular, shallow open tanks. Water flowed through constantly and the mixture was stirred, eventually forming a claylike product. After it dried, it was placed in a kiln to burn off chemicals and other residues, leaving the silver. The vast, work-intensive process covered acres. At San Miguel, most of the processing tanks now lie under water and the huge chimneys of the kilns stand in rigid silence (Fig. 5.17). The cut stone piers and arches which carried the tremendous quantities of water required for ore processing are the essence of design simplicity (Fig. 5.18). San Miguel de Regla is a masterpiece of engineering and a prime example of early industrial architecture in Mexico. Today San Miguel Regla is a quiet hotel.

PUEBLOS

The cities of Nueva España totaled only about three dozen; pueblos numbered in the thousands and most had a church. Only on rare occasions during this transitional period from the mid-seventeenth to the mid-eighteenth century did the professional architect work in the pueblos. The local builder or sculptor, trying to emulate the city

FIGURE 5.17. San Miguel Regla: settling tanks, kiln chimneys.

FIGURE 5.18. San Miguel Regla: aqueduct arches.

FIGURE 5.19. Atlixco: Blessed Sacrament chapel, facade, second tier.

styles, displayed not only individual skills but, more important, the tastes and values of his community.[15] Certain pueblos in the states of Puebla, Morelos, Oaxaca, and Zacatecas offer some of Mexico's most interesting examples of the vernacular in which personal expression outweighs formal training, particularly in sculpture.

FIGURE 5.20. Atlixco: Third Order of Saint Francis church, west front and facade.

FIGURE 5.21. Tonantzintla: church facade,
detail of tile work.

ATLIXCO (Puebla)

A few miles southwest of the city of Puebla, Atlixco boasts several
seventeenth-century structures noted for their excellent designs in
stucco. Two of these structures, a tiny chapel and a small church, will
be described.

Next to the church of La Merced, located on the plaza, is the
chapel of Christ, dedicated to the Blessed Sacrament. Stucco vegeta-
tion surrounding the second-level window is almost organic, especially
the solomonic columns which have been transformed into thick stalks,
tightly interwoven (Fig. 5.19). Above the window, reaching from the

drum into the dome, a consecrated Host is displayed in a monstrance whose golden rays form a pinwheel of fireworks. Archangels stand atop two serious-faced lions holding a quaint version of the royal double-headed eagle.

Nearby is the small church of the Third Order of Saint Francis. The paired columns of the facade resemble the twisted solomonic style, but little else is traditional (Fig. 5.20). The artist's individuality bursts forth in the second level, where a profusion of designs surround a shell window, and mermaids with vegetal bodies float gracefully at the sides. The tiny figure in the third level calls attention to the brooding face enveloped in swags just above the keystone of the portal. Diffusion is constrained by the curved upper frame. This facade was fashioned entirely with mortar by a master not trained in the academic prescriptions for sculpture popular at that time.

TONANTZINTLA (Puebla)

The small church in Tonantzintla, also near the city of Puebla, is entirely the result of native craftsmanship. Its origins are in the eighteenth century. The facade is dressed entirely in colorful tiles (Fig. 5.21).[16] In the lower tier pairs of broad pilasters occupy the space between outer frame and door. The choir window in the second tier carries a heavy frame flanked by niches with statues. Centered above is a statue of Mary, patroness, so tiny its features and detail are almost indistinguishable. The facade provides no hint of the church's riotous interior.

Surfaces covered with ornamentation are not unusual in Mexico, but those at Tonantzintla are peerless. The view into the crossing and apse overwhelms the eye (and even the camera) (Fig. 5.22). Faces and wings completely cover all surfaces like billowing clouds, causing walls to "disappear" and surfaces to pulse with radiance. To emphasize its load-bearing function, the soffits of an arch usually remain unadorned. Those at Tonantzintla, however, are covered with faces and fronds cast in deep relief (Fig. 5.23). Structural "facts" of edge, surface and support have been eliminated. Not seeing structural elements is bewildering and unnerving.

High overhead in the crown of the lanternless, crossing dome the Trinity is displayed. What would otherwise be ribs, key structural ele-

FIGURE 5.22. Tonantzintla: view into crossing and sanctuary.

FIGURE 5.23. Tonantzintla: soffit of arch.

FIGURE 5.24. Tonantzintla: Saint Matthew in oval frame.

ments, are transformed into twisting streamers, like festooned crepe paper. Interspaces are filled with faces of angels and curled patterns. The area of the pendentive is allocated to the four evangelists. In one, Saint Matthew sits within a heavy oval frame encircled with spirals edged with gold (Fig. 5.24). He is poised to write, his gaze fixed intently, awaiting inspiration. Hair and beard are full, painted light brown; his garments are flowing, in red and blue. To either side, chubby angel faces with curly dark brown hair emerge from four-petaled flowers. At his feet an angel with clenched hands is supporting the frame. Other angels beam happily down upon any onlookers.

In creating the interior of Tonantzintla the anonymous eighteenth-century artist(s) took that "leap of the imagination" characteristic of true artistic expression. Stucco work and painting were done with

FIGURE 5.25. Tepalcingo, Santuario: church, façade, Saint Peter,
Christ in the Garden, to left of door.

FIGURE 5.26. Tepalcingo, Santuario: church, facade, Saint Paul, blindfolded Christ, to right of door.

FIGURE 5.27. Tepalcingo, Santuario: church, facade, detail of columns.

verve and audacity; the artist is expressing a very personal image of heaven, one of joyful splendor, filled with song and dance. There is not a single static moment in this artistic display. In the words of Toussaint, "No other (interior) has the Indian flavor of this church: the angels which abound in the decoration are little Indians, as if the Indians knew no other type of beauty to represent."[17]

TEPALCINGO (Morelos)

Nearly all visitors to the santuario in Tepalcingo are pilgrims.[18] In spite of, or perhaps because of, many years of litigation between the bishop and the pastor over the processional rights of its renowned statue of a fallen Christ carrying the cross, the popularity of Tepalcingo's statue grew. The present santuario was built between 1759 and 1782.

Architecturally, the cruciform church is not unusual. Sculpturally, its facade has no equal. Its purpose was meant to be didactic, since many episodes from the life and death of Christ are depicted. The tall rectangular facade is set so deeply between tower bases that it allows for a folding screen composition comprising three horizontal tiers and five vertical divisions.

Amidst a welter of images the drama unfolds section by section. First to be examined are those to either side of the door. Immediately capturing one's attention is the high relief statue of Saint Peter in the section to the left of the door (Fig. 5.25). Angels hold back heavy curtains allowing mortals to view him holding the keys to the Kingdom of Heaven. In the niche above is a scene from the Agony in the Garden, an angel succoring Christ. (The sleeping apostles are found on the outer [perpendicular] panel, partially seen on the far left.) Figures and flora emerge from bulbous columns. Adam lies asleep in the capital of the doorjamb; opposite, on the right jamb, Eve gazes at the forbidden fruit (Fig. 5.26). On this side, mirroring Saint Peter, Saint Paul stands under the blindfolded Christ. The large figures on the four columns are the four evangelists with their respective symbols. At the base of the farthest right column is a heart sprouting flowers; its

FIGURE 5.28. Tepalcingo, Santuario: church, facade, keystone, scenes from Last Supper, mocked Christ.

mirror image to the left of the door is pierced with swords. Are the sprouting flowers long-remembered sacred imagery from prehispanic times? The large dimensions of these columns and the plasticity of their figures is revealed in this detail (Fig. 5.27).

Above the arched door frame and filling the spandrels, angels hold a cloth which forms the keystone (Fig. 5.28). A frieze stretching across three divisions of the facade is devoted to the Last Supper. In the center, Christ holds bread and a chalice. To either side are four apostles; the other eight are located in the adjoining panels. Above, in the niche, the mocked Christ is seated, a wreath of thorns on his head, a cloak thrown over his shoulders. On both sides of the niche a flat floral pattern, fronted with squat square columns, stretches across the facade. An occasional angel floats downward.

In the middle tier other scenes from Christ's passion are depicted (Fig. 5.29). Here undulating columns are intertwined, more organic than structural. Their pattern of sinuous lines and drilled holes makes them almost serpentine. The scene in the crest completes the iconography (Fig. 5.30). In the center is Christ crucified, with Mary Magdalen at his feet; Mary, his mother, to his right; John to his left; and, to each side of Christ, the crucified thieves. At top center, God the Father blesses the Son with his right hand; the left holds a globe, symbolizing the universe.

While Adam and Eve are depicted still in their state of innocence, their fall into sin is clearly implied, since the overriding theme of the figured facade is mankind's redemption from eternal death. If thoughts and intentions behind this work were European, the execution was not. The native artist simply called on his experience and told the story, putting it together as a great piece of popular art. This facade, while echoing the didactic facades of Romanesque Europe, cannot be imagined in eighteenth-century Europe.

NILTEPEC (Oaxaca)

The pueblo of Niltepec is located on the isthmus of Mexico, in the southernmost reaches of Oaxaca. The church of Santiago Apóstol has been dated to at least 1717. More like a chapel, it is only 18.5 meters long with a width of 8.5 meters. The facade (Fig. 5.31) is set only slightly behind the plane of diminutive belfried towers. Three arched

FIGURE 5.29. Tepalcingo, Santuario: church, facade, middle tier, scenes from Christ's passion.

lobes spanning the wide door are fringed with "feathers." Immediately above, at least seven "geometric" designs are raised in sharp, high relief. These are set within their own curved frame above which, in the spandrels, are "rays." Pairs of helicoid columns, with indeterminate capitals, frame two niches to each side. In the "broken" entablature the frieze is filled with designs in high relief, some of them apparently floral. The projecting cornice rests upon a base covered with triangular designs. The surface of the crest, topped with loops, is punctured by two oval openings and a deep cut niche, the rest covered with winged angel faces and cross-shaped high reliefs. No academically correct facade possesses such spontaneity and joyfulness. This enchanting example of eighteenth-century "folk art" by an unknown artist is as Mexican as tortillas.

FIGURE 5.30. Tepalcingo, Santuario: church, facade, crest, Crucifixion scene, God the Father at top.

FIGURE 5.31. Niltepec: church, facade.

FIGURE 5.32. Huitepec: church, west front, atrio wall, posas.

HUITEPEC (Oaxaca)

A perfectly proportioned atrio (34 by 36 meters) with single-opening posas is placed to the west of the 35-meter church of San Antonio Huitepec (Fig. 5.32). Robust stone tower bases, almost four meters square, flank the white ten-meter facade which bears the indistinct date "17_ _". Above the facade door an elaborate octagonal choir window is set within a columned frame (Fig. 5.33). On its cornice rest three candelabralike objects in relief, flanked by empty niches with frames only half as tall as that of the window. In the crest, made of a series of curves, three smaller candelabra branch out into nine arms.

The long, narrow nave (7 by 26 meters), closed with a shed roof of sheet metal over open rafters, has no bays and only four windows (Fig. 5.34). The walls are painted blue. New square tie beams sit on corbels next to what appear to be the originals. If these are indeed the original corbels, then these "anchors" indicate the original ceiling consisted of timbers set in the polygonal shape characteristic of sixteenth-century ceilings.

The church itself may be much older than its eloquent eighteenth-century scalloped facade. Do the nine arms of the candelabra still

FIGURE 5.33. Huitepec: church, facade, octagonal choir window.

FIGURE 5.34. Huitepec: view from rear into sanctuary, wooden ceiling.

have reference to the prehispanic sacred number nine? Most striking is the atrio with posas arranged for processions turning to the right upon leaving the church, a strong reminder of the persistence of sixteenth-century traditions. The complex presents a very harmonious composition.

SOMBRERETE (Zacatecas)

Though close to the road linking Zacatecas and Durango, Sombrerete does not attract the traveler even though it retains its colonial air. As early as 1570 both religious and secular clergy were resident. Silver mining began in earnest in 1645, reaching its apogee in the eighteenth century. Four of Sombrerete's seven churches are from this epoch.

Begun around 1740, Santa Cruz was consecrated in 1754. Although parts are missing, the facade is clearly composed as three tiers (Fig. 5.35). Only the lowest is divided into three verticals. In the second tier the choir window is defined by columns; in the third the soli-

FIGURE 5.35. Sombrerete, Santa Cruz: church, facade.

FIGURE 5.36. Sombrerete, Santa Cruz: church, facade, lower tier.

tary niche has only its frame. To accommodate the great height of the portal, paired columns, framing a niche with statue, are on very high pedestals.

The bottom tier retains an original freshness (Fig. 5.36). The columns are not solomonic even though the entwined grapevine suggests that appearance. Tiny blossoms are "stamped out" in the face of the arch. Flowers filling the spandrels and frieze are cut much deeper though still flat-edged. Directly over the keystone a small cartouche carries the date "AD 74" (i.e., 1774). Style alone would have suggested the eighteenth century. The unknown but highly skilled stone carver of Santa Cruz's facade was probably influenced by the parish church/cathedral in Zacatecas, whose facade was completed by 1745.

In the eighteenth century the single nave, cruciform, vaulted church is common in the pueblos of Mexico. The churches in several Oaxaca pueblos merit attention as distinctive works of architecture for this century.

FIGURE 5.37. Tayata: Santa Cruz, apse wall with semicircular structure at center.

TAYATA (Oaxaca)

Santa Catarina Tayata and Santa Cruz Tayata are like sister pueblos. Santa Catarina dates from 1711, Santa Cruz from 1731. Though both churches are small, their significance lies in certain unique features.

Measuring over 11 meters, the straight rear apse wall of Santa Cruz is solid masonry, guarded by huge buttresses at each corner (Fig. 5.37). Protruding from the center of this wall a semicircular stone structure, with a diameter of 2.8 meters, rises in three diminishing stages to the roof line.

Santa Catarina's apse wall terminates in a cluster of half circles extending two meters.[19] This is a unique configuration, perhaps in all of colonial Mexico. Centered on this wall, a squared addition, each side about 2.5 meters in length, rises in three diminishing tiers to the roof line. An inscription identifies it as a camarín whose window was closed on 31 December 1792. This implies that the similar structure on Santa Cruz was also a camarín. Both arms of Santa Catarina's transept are semicircles, their curvature beginning immediately at the nave walls. Over the crossing is a high octagonal drum carrying an octagonal dome with lantern. Another octagonal dome closes the sanctuary. Plans of these two Tayata churches clarify their distinctive architectural aspects (Fig. 5.38).

XANICA (Oaxaca)

Santiago Xanica is a remarkably well-preserved single-nave church with no sign of earthquake damage. Because the church is on a steep mountainside it entailed considerable work to create a flat surface on which to place the atrio and build the church. Brick was used in its construction, presumably because the abundant stone in the area was too difficult to quarry and cut. Documents place construction dates between 1699 and 1803. A small atrio is well defined but not walled.

The exterior of the rectangular church measures 38 by 9.5 meters. Buttresses and lanterned domes clearly define six divisions (Fig. 5.39). The dome over the fifth bay is larger than the others. The

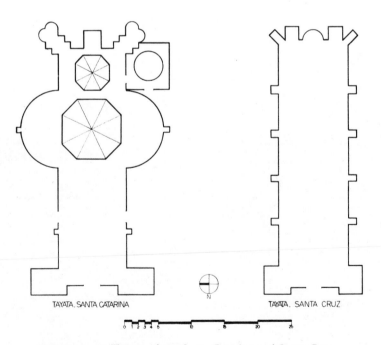

TAYATA. SANTA CATARINA

TAYATA. SANTA CRUZ

FIGURE 5.38. Tayata: plans: Santa Catarina and Santa Cruz.

dimensions of the apse, 6 meters deep and 9.5 wide, cause that dome to be ovoid.

Entrance to the choir is by exterior stairs on the north nave (Fig. 5.40). What was apparently a door in the second bay is now closed. The extension from the fifth bay is a sacristy, not a transept arm. Belfries, bases, walls, and buttresses, made almost entirely of brick, were fashioned by skilled hands. Domes are likely to be brick laid in diminishing circles and covered with a plaster seal. The facade is cast in a sober classical mode, which places its construction around 1800. Except for the portal, there is no sign that the all-brick west front (14 meters) has ever been covered with stucco.

The nave, consisting of the choir and four rectangular bays, measures 29.5 meters in length. The interior has been "modernized" and the colonial furnishings replaced. Green and white plastic garlands adorn the entire nave. Each bay (Fig. 5.41) is formed by arches rising from broad piers and closed with a domical vault. The span of the nave

FIGURE 5.39. Xanica: view of church from north.

is 6.5 meters. Between the piers are arched niches four meters wide, their depth adding another meter to the span. Santiago's six large domes represent a strikingly imaginative design. Their interiorized buttressing constitutes an extraordinary technical accomplishment.

COMALTEPEC (Oaxaca)

Comaltepec is no longer the prosperous community that built its exemplary church. Though a church in this pueblo can be documented to the sixteenth century, the present one belongs to the eighteenth century, in all likelihood after Comaltepec became a secular parish in 1706–1707 and was elevated to a benefice in 1722.

San Juan is a large, cruciform church with an overall length of 43 meters with only a small atrio. The facade faces east, the entire wall having a width of 16.6 meters. The 9.2-meter brick facade is set deep within protecting tower bases (Fig. 5.43). Statues fill all six niches,

FIGURE 5.40. Xanica: church, north nave wall, lanterned domes, steps to choir.

FIGURE 5.41. Xanica: view toward choir (north nave wall)
from bay nearest sanctuary.

tightly enframed with heavy engaged fluted columns and projecting
entablatures. Between the tall arched door and octagonal choir window the patron, Saint John the Baptist, is enshrined in a small niche.
High on the facade "de 71" (i.e., 1771) is inscribed. The two belfries,
crowned with fine iron crosses, have corners of bundled slender
columns which project beyond the plane of their massive 3.7-by-3.7
bases, an unusual configuration (Fig. 5.42).

The high mampostería south-nave wall is only 17.5 meters long
but graced with a strongly articulated and beautifully sculpted portal
(Fig. 5.44). Broad, paneled pilasters, capped with pyramidal finials,
rise from base to entablature, breaking the lines of the arched doorway capitals. Between them a tall niche with its own pilasters and
entablature houses a statue. All flat surfaces are covered in light relief.
Near the top of the wall, S-shaped stones, repeating the S theme
carved on the main door, frame a circular "escutcheon."

Transept arms, only 4 meters deep, are considerably shorter than
the 10-meter west terminus (Fig. 5.45). An undulating parapet
graced with merlons conceals the apse and transept vaulting. Lobed
windows are high on the end walls of the transept arms and the side
walls of the apse. Four windows pierce the base of the drumless cross-

FIGURE 5.42.
Comaltepec: north
tower belfry with
bundled columns.

FIGURE 5.43.
Comaltepec: church,
east wall, facade.

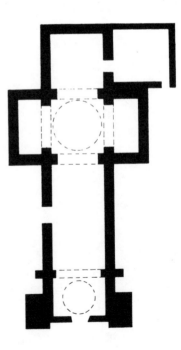

FIGURE 5.44.
Comaltepec: portal,
south nave.

FIGURE 5.45.
Comaltepec: apse
(west wall), crossing
dome, from southwest.

FIGURE 5.46.
Comaltepec: church, plan.

FIGURE 5.47 (opposite
page). Comaltepec: view
into crossing dome and
south transept.

ing dome which is crowned with a blind lantern and the ubiquitous loudspeaker. The north-nave wall does not have a door. High in the north transept is the date 1782, probably signifying completion of repairs.

Seen in plan (Fig. 5.46), the distinctive design of San Juan, with measurements of 43 meters by 16 for the nave, by 24 for the transept, emphasizes the massive towers, a short undelineated nave, long shallow transepts and a deep apse. Such a plan supports an eighteenth-century origin. A barrel vault closes the nave, defined only by arches at either end. An opening in the center of the nave vault provides a source of light. The choir loft, sustained by a vault and suppressed arches, has a window high in the wall. Floors are brick.

A retablo completely fills the terminal wall of the deep raised sanctuary, also closed with a barrel vault. At the crossing pendentives carry the closed dome (Fig. 5.47). The shallow barrel-vaulted transept arms have windows in the lunettes. A strong cornice runs the length of the entire interior, unifying the design.

SUGGESTED READING

Baird, Joseph A. *The Churches of Mexico, 1530–1810.* University of California Press, 1962.

———. "Mexican Architecture and the Baroque," *International Congress of the History of Art, XX, New York, 1961.* Princeton University Press, 1963, 191–202.

Gibson, Charles. *The Aztecs under Spanish Rule: A History of the Valley of Mexico: 1519–1810.* Stanford University Press, 1964.

Mexico: Splendors of Thirty Centuries. The Metropolitan Museum of Art, 1990, 315–356.

Weismann, Elizabeth. *Art and Time in Mexico.* Harper & Row, 1985; Icon edition, 1995, 195–219.

6

The Age of Fulfillment, 1730–1800: Estípites, "Silver" Churches, Santuarios, Residences

⊷ ⊱◈⊰ ⊶

B Y the early eighteenth century, Nueva España's economy had recovered. Economic power, once vested solely with crown and church, was now shared by the private sector, resulting primarily in replacement of the *encomienda* system with the *repartimiento*. This, together with the growth of merchandising and mining, created a new class of wealth. Rich silver lodes were discovered, especially in northern Mexico, and private mine owners suddenly found themselves immensely rich.

From this new economic power base a new social structure emerged, the *patronazgo*. This charitable and religious institution functioned on a legal basis with contracts signed and witnessed before an ecclesiastical notary. Members of the patronazgo became patrons of art. They had a voice in the selection of architects, sculptors, and artists, and their donations resulted in many large, richly adorned churches. In return the patrons were granted certain privileges, including the right to burial within the church. Most significant to architecture is that assured patronage allowed construction of the entire church and all its furnishings within a short span. It was otherwise rare in colonial Mexico to see a church with a single, unified style. This architecture was essentially of the city, or at least the urban area. Stylistic origins were based in Mexico City.

CATHEDRAL (Mexico City)

"The Ultra-Baroque style, which the Mexicans call Churrigueresque, was brought in by an extremely gifted designer from Seville, Jerónimo de Balbás. . . . "[1] For nineteen years he labored on the huge new retablo for the Cathedral (Fig. 6.1). The *Altar de Los Reyes* was completed in 1737, emerging a true masterpiece and ushering in a new artistic era. Incredibly intricate, the retablo is a tour de force of wood carving, so complex and lustrous in gold leaf that it dazzles the eye. Architectural lines are lost in the profusion of deeply-cut ornamentation covering every surface. Balbás dared to create, in large scale sculpture, the estípite, a "column" square in plan with tapered bottom and formed of several sections, giving the appearance of stacked parts. The lower half of the Cathedral's estípite is squared, tapering at the base like an inverted obelisk, and has a capital located about midpoint. The upper half is a series of cubes with capitals, abstract motifs, foliage, and putti. A boldly projecting cornice divides the retablo from the apse dome. Of the two oil paintings placed on the center axis of the retablo, the lower one depicts the Adoration of the Three Kings (hence the retablo's name) and the upper one, the Assumption. This retablo "signalled the start of a new era in Mexican colonial architecture that many consider the most brilliant flowering of the Andalusian retablo style."[2]

SAGRARIO (Mexico City)

The *Altar de los Reyes* was the immediate inspiration for the facade of the Sagrario, the Cathedral's parish church.[3] Such a church existed next to this Cathedral since at least 1603, but the present structure was built between 1749 and 1768 by another Andalusian, Lorenzo Rodríguez. The interior, a Greek-cross plan (equilateral arms), is itself unusual, but in creating the facade this architect set out to accomplish in stone what Balbás had created in wood—and succeeded!

FIGURE 6.1. Mexico City, Cathedral, Altar de los Reyes (1737) (Instituto de Investigaciones Estéticas, Universidad Nacional Autónoma de México, México).

FIGURE 6.2. Mexico City: Sagrario, main facade of parish church
(Instituto de Investigaciones Estéticas,
Universidad Nacional Autónoma de México, México).

FIGURE 6.3. Mexico City: Sagrario, facade, detail, paired estípites.

Tightly compressed within slender frames of gray chiluca stone, an array of estípites dances before the eye (Fig. 6.2). Light flickers over countless facets. So prismatic is the effect, so strong are the verticals, that the whole facade seems about to launch itself into space. By careful inspection the regular three vertical zones and three horizontal tiers can be seen, although the crest is little more than finials. By inserting recessed "columns" between the estípites, Rodríguez ornamented every inch of his facade, and set a new precedent. Paired estípites replace paired classic-order columns (Fig. 6.3). Where once columns framed a statue in a fairly large niche, estípites virtually conceal the sculptured figure. Figures and faces are strewn over the facade, some so small they are barely visible. Dynamism replaces demarcation. The white shimmer of the facade is daringly contrasted with the subdued glow of tezontle side walls, resembling tempered bronze.

A bold, new, provocative facade had been created. This was the ultimate in sculptural virtuosity—exuberance in stone. A new architectural style emerged. For the rest of the century the estípite became the dominant motif in church architecture.

TEPOTZOTLÁN (México State)

The church at Tepotzotlán was begun by the Jesuits in 1670 and dedicated to San Francisco Javier (Saint Francis Xavier) in 1682. The Franciscans had earlier established a school for Indians, named San Martín. Under the Jesuits this school became an important seminary, and the original name was largely forgotten. Its eleven dazzling gilded retablos constitute one of the prime examples of seventeenth-century retablo art. Its camarín is a jewel of the seventeenth-century Mexican Baroque. Weismann describes it as a "total ensemble—all coherent, proportionate, harmonious—an exemplar of the perfection we dream of . . . it is a perfect world—a Paradise—in small."[4]

Construction of the facade took place between 1760 and 1762 (Fig. 6.4). The asymmetry of the single belfry is its foremost distinction. The left frame of the facade seems weak compared to the sturdy tower base framing the right side. Horizontals uniting facade and frames have a quieting effect, and steady cornices create unmistakable tiers of almost equal height. The verticals are solidly contained by the

FIGURE 6.4.
Tepotzotlán:
church facade.

cornices. With no intercolumniation, Tepotzotlán's estípites function as frames for the niches and statues, thereby emphasizing them. The large óculo of Tepotzotlán's facade gives it a standard, even conservative, appearance. Its crest makes an unchallengeable statement as the third tier.

Tepotzotlán possesses an illustrious retablo facade whose detail immediately reveals superb artistry (Fig. 6.5). Luxuriant foliage adorns the estípite. Beneath this and inside swirling frames, small realistic figures express various moods. Above, a commanding angel, whose face is filled with wondrous expectation, alights with garments rippling in the wind and right hand resting lightly on a scroll, as if to gain balance. The scrolls are delicate, lines precise, and moldings gently curved. This designer/sculptor remains anonymous.

Nationalized by President Carranza (1917–1920), the entire com-

FIGURE 6.5. Tepotzotlán: church facade, detail, estípite.

plex was restored in 1964. It now contains several museums, housing a superb collection of art created during the Viceregency.

GUANAJUATO (Guanajuato)

Silver mines located in the state of Guanajuato were particularly productive during the eighteenth century. Many churches and monuments in that state owe their origin to the patronazgo. Most impressive are those in the capital, Guanajuato, which was founded in 1552 and continues to offer exceptional charm and enchanting vistas. Among its "silver" churches are La Compañía, San Francisco, San Diego, and San Juan de Rayas. Another "silver" church just outside this Royal City of Mines owes its existence to the Valenciana Mine.

On a small hill near the mine's entrance stands the parish church, San Cayetano, built between 1765 and 1788 by a patronazgo member, the wealthy Count of Valenciana. The church is grandiose; it overwhelms the small pueblo in which it is found. From entrance to apse the interior measures 40 meters. The width of the single nave is 9.8 meters; a transept and dome augment its stature.

The architect designed the rectangle of the entire front, tower bases and facade, as a single composition (Fig. 6.6). As a result, San Cayetano presents one of the most unified facades of colonial Mexico. The same ashlar is used on the sculptured facade and the slightly projecting bases. Each tower base has three shadowed openings of different shapes and sizes, topped with the solid faces of clocks. This cadence serves as a steady counterpoint to the vibrant lines of the facade. The majestic curve over the choir window is the critical unifying factor. If this curve were extended, it would come to rest on the sills of the center windows in the tower bases. This subtle linkage between facade and bases is unequivocally assured by the cornice which firmly binds both together.

The very slim and tall facade displays a thoroughly integrated design. The usual three verticals and three horizontals are so subsumed within the overall design that they are virtually imperceptible. Slender estípites rush upward, their thrust finally being halted by a serrated cornice creating a deep shadow. This shadow line is raised in the center where the cornice becomes the sill of the choir window. Between sill and portal a small compact relief depicts angels hovering over the Trinity, the three figures seated over a globe. The heavy curved cornice closing the second tier is "supported" by slender estípites and flanked by empty niches. The rectangular choir window reiterates the tower base windows. A tall, flamelike crest accents the center axis of the entire design.

Eight windows in the drum of the dome flood the transept arms, crossing, and apse with light. Side windows in the apse also bring light to the resplendent retablo in the sanctuary (Fig. 6.7). If it were possible to detach the facade, without its crest, and push it back through the nave into the apse, it would closely match the retablo. The outer estípites of the retablo are "normal" in their thickness, providing visual support to the heavy arch framing the retablo. The inner estípites, however, are as thin as those of the facade. In both the emphasis is directed to the intercolumns. Statues make the retablo more complete than the facade. The large arch in the center has the same dimensions as the portal. Instead of the Trinity relief, the retablo has a niche, occupied by the patron, Saint Cayetano of Siena. In the place given to the choir window in the facade, the retablo has a statue of Mary and Child surrounded by angels. La Valenciana's unity of style in both the interior and the exterior constitutes a brilliant manifestation of one of Guanajuato's many "silver churches."

TAXCO (Guerrero)

José de la Borda exemplified the patronazgo.[5] By donating close to one million pesos for the construction and furnishing of the church of Santa Prisca and San Sebastián he was empowered to sign the contract with the architect, Cayetano de Sigüenza, and to commission Isidoro Vicente de Balbás to carve the main retablo and eight others. This church was built in the remarkably short time of seven years (1751–1758). Borda thereby fulfilled his well-known avowal, "God has given to Borda and Borda gives to God." Although damaged during the civil strife in the early decades of the twentieth century, Santa Prisca has been restored with great faithfulness to the original.

After the old church was demolished (earliest baptismal records date to 1621), a large, stone foundation was built level with the plaza, raising the east side 6 meters above street level. Oriented east-west, the plan of Santa Prisca is the usual Latin cross, but with several distinctive features (Fig. 6.8). The perimeter walls constitute a rectangle, twice as long as it is wide. The north wall protrudes to provide sufficient width for the rectangular chapel, known as "La Capilla de los Naturales." The only entrance to this chapel is from the nave. On the equivalent part of the south wall is a portal giving access to a baptistry and archives. The fourth nave bay is located outside the rectangle, set between the deep tower bases. The immense crossing is not a square, its width a meter greater than its length. Walls, as thick as those of the nave, form the sanctuary and adjoining rooms. Between the sanctuary and terminal east wall are two sacristies.

The proportions of the west front are remarkable. Enclosing the tall belfries and their bases within an imaginary line, a rectangle is

FIGURE 6.6. Guanajuato (Valenciana): San Cayetano, west front.

FIGURE 6.7. Guanajuato (Valenciana): view into sanctuary, retablo.

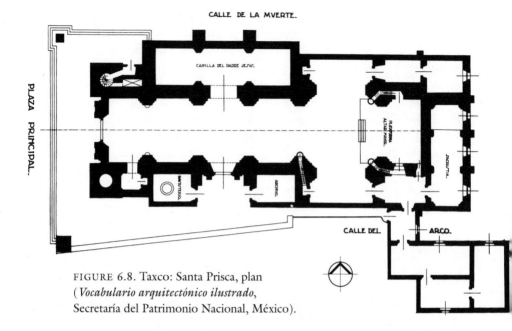

FIGURE 6.8. Taxco: Santa Prisca, plan
(*Vocabulario arquitectónico ilustrado,*
Secretaría del Patrimonio Nacional, México).

formed that is twice as high as it is wide (Fig. 6.9). Tower bases are as tall as the belfries. The striking ϒ format of the ornamentation brings to mind arms uplifted in jubilation. This unity of design is carried out ingeniously in the lower half of the rectangle. The eight piercings in the slender tower bases contrast sharply with the deep-set facade. The "three-by-three" format is still employed but handled so adroitly that it looks as if there were only two tiers. In the second tier Saint Prisca and Saint Sebastian, the patron saints, pose inside shallow niches framed by paired twisted columns (Fig. 6.10). While cornices enclose this frame they do not close the second tier. The choir window links the second and third tiers as does a curved cornice which blends the two together.

Vertically from the base of the facade the architect aligned a very tall door, the papal coat of arms (in anticipation of a never-received designation of basilica), a large relief in an oval frame, the choir window, a shell design, a clock, and a statue of Mary as the finial. The large relief (Fig. 6.11) depicts the baptism of Christ by John the Baptist in the river Jordan, with the Trinity above. The towers seem burdened with sculpture. Bells hang in all eight piercings, each framed

FIGURE 6.9. Taxco: church, west front (Instituto de Investigaciones Estéticas, Universidad Nacional Autónoma de México, México).

FIGURE 6.10. Taxco: facade with Saint Prisca and Saint Sebastian (Instituto de Investigaciones Estéticas, Universidad Nacional Autónoma de México, México).

FIGURE 6.11. Taxco: facade, central relief, Baptism of Christ (Instituto de Investigaciones Estéticas, Universidad Nacional Autónoma de México, México).

with engaged columns. Estípites occupy corners of the lower belfries. This remarkable ensemble is a rich offering, meant to be relished at leisure. Despite the rich complexity of its composition, it is more at rest than restless, more calm than dynamic.

The son of Jerónimo, Isidoro Vicente de Balbás clearly had in mind his father's great work, *The Altar de los Reyes*, when he created the sanctuary's retablo (Fig. 6.12). This dynamic creation is almost in frenzy as every line leaps upward like crackling flames. On the center axis, starting from the bottom, are: altar, tabernacle, a large statue of Mary enclosed in glass, the Sacred Heart of Jesus, the segmental curve of the cornice with a pope seated on each slope, a large statue of Saint Peter, and, at the very top, God the Father. Gigantic estípites, climbing vigorously from floor to cornice, proclaim inter-columns with many figures of angels, saints, and popes. On the left side of the center is Saint Prisca; on the right, Saint Sebastian. Above the broken cornice tightly paired estípites rise to another cornice framing the niche in which Saint Peter stands, its curve fitting snugly

FIGURE 6.12. Taxco: retablo in sanctuary (Instituto de Investigaciones Estéticas, Universidad Nacional Autónoma de México, México).

FIGURE 6.13. Ocotlán, Santuario: west front from atrio gate.

into the curvature of the vault. The depth of the retablo increases discreetly and almost imperceptibly with height. A plumb line dropped from the top would strike the floor almost two meters away from the base.

There is a profound difference in spirit between retablo and facade. Balbás and Sigüenza possessed distinctive artistic temperaments. Perhaps Borda realized this when he contracted for their services. Santa Prisca is an incomparable legacy, an exemplary statement of mid-eighteenth century architecture of colonial Mexico.[6] Weismann declared it to be "The most perfect ensemble of them all [Mexican Baroque]—the purest and the most complete. . . ."[7] In this period the "retablo church" reached its florescence.

OCOTLÁN (Tlaxcala)

Ocotlán is the hilltop site of a santuario affording a marvelous view of the city of Tlaxcala. Here a statue of the Virgin, Our Lady of Ocotlán, is venerated. According to legend, she was discovered in the trunk of a tree around 1540, then long housed in a small chapel. Ever larger pilgrimage groups over the years created the demand for a more fitting shrine. Sometime in the last half of the eighteenth century her new church was completed, and it remains a popular pilgrimage destination.

From the atrio gate, an incredible sight greets the eye (Fig. 6.13). The snow-white, turbulent surface of the facade is wedged between bright-red, stalwart tower bases. The mathematical precision of the hexagonal tile pattern offsets the restless strivings of the facade. Two-tiered, white-encrusted belfries reach for the heavens, climbing upward like white cumulus clouds. A curved shell closing the facade links the whole into a unified design. The star-shaped óculo becomes a spectacular setting for the small stone replica of Our Lady of Ocotlán—a stunning creation!

In the lower tier, paired free-standing estípites, replete with flora and figures, frame intercolumns with life-size figures (Fig. 6.14). The pictured angel is made from stucco formed around an armature, as seen in the broken right arm of the angel. Above is the bust of a pope, to the sides, doctors of the Church—each vibrantly lifelike. Annual applications of whitewash keep resplendent the perishable stucco forming this lively scene.

After the choir nave, the single nave opens into three bays (Fig. 6.15). The nave is quite wide, almost 15 meters, but dimly lit since windows are small and above the spring of the rectangular vaults. In the fourth bay nave walls curve inward to form a triumphal arch, transformed into a huge shell whose lip extends back nearly to the third bay. The 9-meter crossing, closed with an octagonal dome set on a drum, is flanked by transepts so shallow they scarcely extend beyond the nave walls. The sanctuary has the same width as the crossing, but only half its depth. The end wall opens into an octagonal chamber, the camarín. This wall is covered with a magnificent retablo, its gold sheath shimmering in the filtered light from the small vault lantern. Light levels within the church remain low. The ambiance of this interior covered with gold and bathed in the soft light is enthralling. Interiors like this "seem almost miraculously harmonious. They strike the senses like a rich chord of music. One can look at the detail and enjoy it or criticize it; but one cannot argue with the whole."[8]

High in the retablo is an aperture, shaped like the facade's óculo. Here, presented for viewing, stands the famed statue of Our Lady of Ocotlán. When the statue requires new robes and jewels, it is carried down into the camarín by means of a short, narrow stairway permanently fixed in that room. This camarín is a 10-meter octagon, covered with a lanterned dome (Fig. 6.16). Seven of the eight sides are covered with paintings depicting traditional scenes from the Life of the Virgin. They are the work of Juan de Villalobos. One of them is signed and dated 1723, a generation earlier than the post-1750 facade. All other surfaces are lavishly covered with looped bands, garlands, and angels—masterpieces of stucco sculpture.

CHAPEL OF EL POCITO (Villa Madero, Mexico City)

Near the santuario of Our Lady of Guadalupe is another devotional site, small but of surpassing beauty and charm. The Chapel of El Pocito now shelters a well, its waters long given curative powers. Designed by the architect Francisco de Guerrero y Torres, the chapel was built between 1777 and 1791 as a large oval with extensions on its east-west axis (Fig. 6.17). This axis measures 30 meters; the north-south axis, 17 meters. The interior of the oval, on the same axes,

FIGURE 6.14. Ocotlán, Santuario: facade, detail.

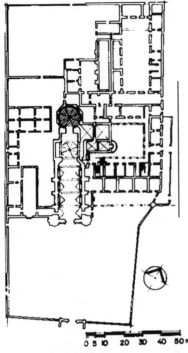

FIGURE 6.15. Ocotlán, Santuario: plan (*Vocabulario arquitectónico ilustrado*, Secretaría del Patrimonio Nacional, México).

FIGURE 6.16. Ocotlán, Santuario: Our Lady of Ocotlán's dressing room, the camarín.

FIGURE 6.17 (opposite, top). Mexico City, Villa de Guadalupe: "El Pocito," plan (*Vocabulario arquitectónico ilustrado*, Secretaría del Patrimonio Nacional, México).

FIGURE 6.18 (opposite, bottom). Villa de Guadalupe: general view, tezontle walls, tiled dome.

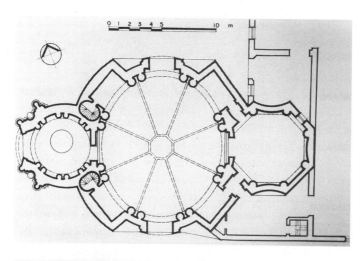

stretches 11.5 by 13 meters. Six separate sections surround this central oval: four chapels honor the Virgin's apparitions to Juan Diego, one serves as the high altar, and one, the entrance, gives cover to the well. Their junctions with the oval are such that their interiors seem to flow into the larger space. These interpenetrating, unobstructed, three-dimensional spaces are the most Baroque, the most "Borrominian" in Mexico!

The exterior is utterly captivating (Fig. 6.18). Walls are tezontle, framed in thin strips of white stone. High in each section is a relatively small star-burst window, also framed in white, thus creating an interplay between straight and curved lines. The curved entrance is a dazzling composite of classical columns, both star-shaped and narrow windows, and surfaces covered with stucco. "The elegance and sensitivity of the sculpture on the main doorway is so moving that we are shaken by its beauty every time we look at it."[9] Parapet and dome are covered with white and blue tiles in a zigzag pattern, thereby emphasizing the egg-shaped dome. Glistening in the sun, El Pocito looks like a crown of jewels.

VARIATIONS

Liberation from the limitations of the classical column had great appeal to both architect and artisan during the last half of the eighteenth century. The estípite emerged in great variety, limited only by the sculptor's imagination. The church of San Francisco can boast of one of the most luxurious estípite facades in Mexico City (Fig. 6.19). Its compressed design displays a singular unity as the vertical accent flows upward to converge in the crest. In the former convento of San Agustín in Querétaro, now a museum, estípites have been transformed into caryatids (Fig. 6.20), shown as youths from the waist up (the pipe extruding from the mouth is a rain spout). Their arms reach up toward the cornice as each hand holds thumb and first finger closed in a loop and the other three fingers extended upwards. San Francisco in Puebla has an entirely different rhythm (Fig. 6.21). The pilasterlike estípites of its facade are mounted atop each other in three tiers of equal size. Set in red brick, fourteen tile panels flanking the facade emphasize its exceptional height and narrowness.

Like the "city" variations, those in the pueblo are equally striking. In Chilac, near the city of Puebla, the designer of San Gabriel's facade

FIGURE 6.19. Mexico City: San Francisco, estípite facade.

FIGURE 6.20. Querétaro:
San Agustín, inner court,
detail, caryatid.

FIGURE 6.21. Puebla:
San Francisco, west front,
facade with estípites.

set his stocky and stacked estípites amidst delicate stucco work (Fig. 6.22). San Francisco Acatepec, also near Puebla, has the distinction of tile estípites. Located in the second and third tiers of the facade, every tile has been fired to fit the specific contour of thirteen estípites (Fig. 6.23). Those flanking the central panel are in groups of three. In the lower tier, fitted tiles follow the curve of the cylinder (Fig. 6.24). These columns are covered with blue-flower-on-white-field tiles, set in an interlocking pattern and juxtaposed against gold-yellow wall tiles. Its entire west front is finished in colored tile from pedestal to pinnacle (Fig. 6.25). Even the solomonic columns of the belfry are fashioned with tiles shaped like a helix.

Acatepec's facade is arranged like a folding screen with sides angling out in front of the tower bases. While its nine sections are clearly delineated in the standard treatment, the central panel appears so hard-pressed by the wings that cornices are broken and "forced" upwards. The segment of a quatrefoil, first stated in the frame of the portal, is repeated in a progressively dynamic manner in each cornice to terminate in the crest. In the third tier the patron, Saint Francis, holds the place of honor. His small statue stands within a quatrefoil set in the cavity of an eight-pointed star. Above him the Trinity is depicted as three young men. San Francisco's west front is both craftsmanship of the highest order and an artistic masterpiece.

The interior is equally extraordinary; it is another Tonantzintla (Chapter 5). Seeing it today one would never suspect that much of the interior was destroyed by fire in 1939. Other than this, little is known about San Francisco Acatepec. Stylistically, the estípites date the second and third tiers of the facade to the late eighteenth century, though the lower tier may be earlier. Yet, considering what happened in the 1940s, the facade could have been the work of later generations. These matters are living traditions.

In the pueblo of Cata, near Guanajuato, its church offers estípites with a variety of layerings dense with floral and geometric design (Fig. 6.26). Their bases taper almost to a point. The facade of the large, ashlar parish church, Santo Tomás in Ixtlán, reflects a style prevalent at that time in the nearby metropole, Oaxaca, when the estípite had not yet reached that city (Fig. 6.27). Spiral columns, jutting, broken-line cornices, and weighty frame surround a superb relief, dated 1757.[10] A few years later the pueblo's parishioners were ready to

FIGURE 6.22. Chilac: San Gabriel, facade, stacked estípites.

FIGURE 6.23. Acatepec: San Francisco, facade, second tier,
detail of tiled estípite.

FIGURE 6.24. San Francisco, facade, detail, tiled lower tier.

FIGURE 6.25. San Francisco, tiled west front.

install the main altar retablo. Then they demanded the latest style. Ixtlán's retablo (Fig. 6.28), repeating the Doubting Thomas scene, is among the finest estípite retablos in Mexico.

RESIDENCES

Private wealth also found expression in fashionable city residences. The custom of building a home in the city was very European. Wealthy landowners were not content to remain on their estates. Wishing to participate in the political, economic and social whirl of the capital or commercial center, they built for themselves large, lavish town houses. This type of noble residence was known in Rome as *palazzo*, in Paris as *hôtel*, in Vienna as *palais* or *Stadthaus*, in London as *town house*. In Mexico City, it was called *palacio*. By the end of the Viceregency that city alone boasted almost forty. All had one thing in common—monumentality. Many still exist.

As customary for all buildings in the cities of Mexico, the palacio fronted directly on the sidewalk. Landscaping in colonial Mexico did not include a front lawn. Privacy was gained within the palacio, which was centered around the patio with its fountain and flowers. The main entrance could be readily identified by height and width (sufficient for carriage passage) and a mass of sculpture. Estípites were often employed as decorative devices. A driveway led to another patio

FIGURE 6.26.
Guanajuato (Cata):
estípite facade.

FIGURE 6.27. Ixtlán: west wall, facade.

FIGURE 6.28. Ixtlán: main retablo with estípites.

from which a grand stairway mounted to spacious upper galleries and living quarters. Guests were formally entertained in a huge salon. Two such palacios in Mexico City will be studied.

The Palacio de Valparaíso, built between 1760 and 1772 by the architect Francisco Guerrero y Torres, is a two-story structure sited on a street corner.[11] Broad panels of light-grey stone and a tower on the third level visually strengthen the corner even while chamfering softens its ridge (Fig. 6.29). The same stone frames the windows. Those on the first floor have metal grilles and, for added security, are set high off the ground. Window frames extend upward to a wide cornice, the panel between filled with relief. The family coat of arms is emblazoned over the portal, placed asymmetrically in the third of eight bays. French doors in the second floor open onto balconies with metal rails. Roof finials accent the verticals created by the spaces between the windows. Ubiquitous rain spouts discharge rainwater well away from the walls. This attractive residence of tezontle ashlars and white stone trim is now occupied by the National Bank of Mexico.

The same bank occupies what is perhaps the grandest town house of colonial Mexico (Fig. 6.30). The former Palacio de Iturbide, also attributed to Francisco Guerrero y Torres, was built in 1780 and became the official residence of the Marquis of Jaral de Berrio.[12] Pronounced cornices divide the structure into three tiers. The lengthy facade is symmetrical, five bays to a side, arranged alternately as solids and voids. Each bay is defined with relief frames. The two at each end are cast as towers to enframe a five-bay arched loggia on the third floor, once without fixed panes of glass. Cornices become balconies with railings.

Pedestrians give scale to the enormous portal (Fig. 6.31). Two-thirds of its 9-meter height consists of the opening. In the panel above is a heavily framed escutcheon in whose center a small head is set in a shell surrounded by twisting, curling leaves. Two flanking Atlantean figures, holding tree trunks, stand on pedestals mounted atop large spirals. Both panel and door have stone frames dense with sculpture, consisting of Ionic pilasters filled with animal faces, putti, mermaids, flowers, fruits, and scrolls. Hard corner edges have been replaced with undulations. Adjoining ground-floor and mezzanine windows are similarly encased in heavily sculpted frames. In contrast, the frames surrounding the large, solid tezontle panels do not protrude but are, instead, incised deeply.

FIGURE 6.29. Mexico City: Palacio de Valparaíso, general view.

The enclosed courtyard is immense (Fig. 6.32). Here the architect faced a challenge. The height of the first level in the courtyard had to match that of the exterior and contain the mezzanine. An original arcade of three arches was changed in 1890 to four. This necessitated placing thin columns on pedestals and "raising" the arches by means of impost blocks set between the capital and the spring. The necessary height was thereby achieved; the rhythm flowed smoothly. Broad stairs lead to the upper floors.

Ground-floor arcades have been transformed into a gallery for art expositions. The main door remains open, a standing invitation to visit the current display. In adapting this edifice to its needs, Banamex was most careful to preserve the stamp of the building's colonial vintage. It succeeded admirably.

In the city of Puebla, the well-to-do adorned their houses, outside and inside, with brick, mortar and tile. Since early colonial days that city had been famous for its tiles, especially glazed tiles (*azulejos*). Many a surface is covered with this durable, colorful ceramic. Among Puebla's imposing colonial residences, one of the most distinguished is the Casa del Alfeñique. This corner town house, in the center of the city, was built toward the end of the eighteenth century by the

FIGURE 6.30.
Mexico City:
Palacio de Iturbide,
general view.

FIGURE 6.31. Palacio
de Iturbide, portal.

FIGURE 6.32. Palacio de Iturbide, inner court (Banamex).

architect Don Antonio de Santa María Incháurregui. Of its three levels, the height of the second is noticeably less than the other two, with a large interior galleried patio (Fig. 6.33). Instead of tezontle exterior walls, this Casa has a facade of brick and tile set in a tightly woven pattern. Rows of glazed tile (pattern blue, background white) contrast with rows of octagonal unglazed terra-cotta brick. The entrance and windows, all carefully aligned, are set in white frames. The stucco work on the third floor and cornice has been applied like frosting (Fig. 6.34). This accounts for its delightful name, The House of Marzipan, "because its delicate and complicated reliefs recall the decoration of the Moorish sweet made of ground almonds and sugar."[13] Glistening, sugary estípites frame the windows on this floor. Taffylike strands of plaster decorate the outside edges. This elegant, tantalizing residence now functions as a museum.

HACIENDAS

In Elizabeth Weismann's view, the eighteenth-century hacienda "had permanently affected the social organization of the viceroyalty . . . " and, as a unit of society, "dominates the history of Mexico." Hacienda architecture, however, did not play nearly such an important role, and these buildings, she continues, "best illustrate the

FIGURE 6.33. Puebla: Casa de Alfeñique, general view.

proposition that architecture is timeless and largely invariable. If it is often impossible to date a granary or a barn, it is even less important to try, since the building and the crop and the animals and the reason for housing them and the people who care for them are all but interchangeable for three centuries."[14]

The end of the Age of Fulfillment was foreshadowed as early as 1781 when the fledgling Royal Academy of San Carlos in Mexico City held its first classes. Charles III approved the establishment of the Royal Academy on 25 December 1783; its official inauguration took place on 4 November 1785. The Academy's professors came from Spain, and the curriculum in architecture, sculpture, and painting followed strictly the precepts of classicism. Profound changes in taste soon followed. The rationalism of neoclassicism with its emphasis on proportion, symmetry, and clean line soon replaced the then free-spirited approach to the arts.

FIGURE 6.34. Casa de Alfeñique, detail, third floor.

SUGGESTED READING

Baird, Joseph A. "Eighteenth Century Retables of the Bajío, Mexico: The Querétaro Style." *Art Bulletin 35*, no. 3 (1953), pp. 195–216.

Hecht, Johanna, "The Liberation of Viceregal Architecture and Design" (pp. 357–360), and Octavio Paz, "Will for Form" (pp. 27–28), *Mexico: Splendors of Thirty Centuries*, The Metropolitan Museum of Art, 1990.

Kelemen, Pál. *Baroque and Rococo in Latin America*. Thomas Y. Crowell, 1969.

Weismann, Elizabeth Wilder. *Art and Time in Mexico*. Harper & Row, 1985; Icon paperback, 1995, pp. 168–194.

7

Frontier Mission Architecture

D URING the sixteenth century several Spanish expeditions explored the heartland of today's United States, bestowing Spanish names on a host of rivers, mountains, and other sites. Actual settlement in Nueva España's northern frontier—today's Southwest—did not take place until don Juan de Oñate formally laid claim to Nuevo México in 1598. In 1610 Santa Fe was made the capital of this region.[1]

By the time Spain's dominion in the New World ended in 1821, the Franciscans and Jesuits had founded hundreds of missions from San Antonio to San Francisco. Their effort, dedication, and spirit were prodigious. Mission churches of this period (many are active parishes) are recognized not only for their historic role but also for their architectural merit.[2] Texas, New Mexico, Arizona, and California have active preservation programs.

TEXAS

The first school in Nueva España whose sole purpose was to train missionaries for the Americas was located in Querétaro. The Colegio de Santa Cruz was established by the Franciscans on 15 August 1683. Shortly thereafter the Franciscans opened another such school in

Zacatecas. During the eighteenth century Franciscans from these two schools established a number of missions between El Paso and East Texas. The earliest missions founded in today's Texas (Tejas) were on the Rio Grande, near El Paso. (The El Paso area was then part of the Province of New Mexico.) Corpus Christi de la Ysleta and Nuestra Señora de la Concepción del Socorro were founded between 1680 and 1682. The earliest mission in East Texas was founded in 1690; several others originated in the early 1700s. These, intended in part to counter the influence of the French in Louisiana, lasted only a few years. The history of the Texas missions is complex. Some were changed in location, others were abandoned; only a few survived the process of secularization through which the autonomous mission became part of the diocesan parish system and its communal land was divided into private property.

The Franciscans who marched northward into Texas in the eighteenth century found themselves among nomadic peoples. In time many of these people were domiciled within the mission complex. The atrio wall suddenly acquired a new function. Not only a perimeter defining a quadrangle, the atrio wall now formed the "outside" wall of Indian homes, built as a continuous series of small dwellings.

"A prevalent misconception is that the mission churches of the Spanish northern borderlands were literally built by their resident ministers . . . [whereas] the evidence from San Antonio de Valero indicates that the ministers attempted to bring professional builders to the borderlands from the outset in order to design and direct the construction of permanent buildings."[3]

SAN ANTONIO

Best known among the mission churches of Texas are the five in San Antonio. Both the Presidio de San Antonio de Béxar and Mission San Antonio de Valero were founded in May 1718.[4] The cornerstone of the mission's cruciform stone church was laid on 8 May 1744. Antonio de Tello had "apparently designed the new church"[5] but was not involved in its construction after 1744. The structure collapsed in 1756, but work continued, as the keystone is dated 1758. An inventory of 1772 mentions a maestro and gives the dimensions of Valero as "35 varas (97') long and 9 (25') wide," very close to the "current length and width of the nave and sanctuary."[6] Today's facade closely fits the 1772 description. Construction was never completed partly because of secularization in 1793–1794.

The "Alamo" (the name given to the church earlier by soldiers) was extensively damaged during the siege of 1836. That struggle, known as the Battle of the Alamo, secured independence for Texas. In 1846 the building was leased from the bishop to the United States Army Quartermaster Corps, which gave it its present well-known silhouette. The Alamo's role as the State's most famous shrine began as early as the 1880s. It received concrete vaults in 1934. Of the original church, only the church walls and facade, minus the curvilinear crest, remain.

Initially all San Antonio missions used "temporary" churches such as those still in existence at Mission San Juan Capistrano and Mission San Francisco de la Espada. Foundations of the never-completed "permanent" churches stand witness. These two missions were established in March 1731 but "we know nothing of the professional craftsmen who were engaged in the planning of these . . . missions."[7] The permanent churches at Mission San José and Mission Concepción are significant architecturally.

In 1719, Fray Antonio Margil de Jesús was a missionary in East Texas. Fleeing the chaotic conditions in that area occasioned by the outbreak of war between Spain and France, large numbers of Indian refugees began to arrive in San Antonio accompanied by Fray Margil. On 23 February 1720, he founded Mission San José y San Miguel de Aguayo, known today as San José, to accommodate these refugees. This mission became the Texas headquarters of the Zacatecas school. The foundations of the present 32.5-by-10-meter limestone church, however, were not laid until 19 May 1768. By 1777 it was reported to be nearly complete. During the intervening years another structure served as the church, probably the 32.5-by-9 barrel-vaulted structure known as the granary. San José was soon known as the "Queen of the Missions" since no other church in Texas could display such elegant statues and intricate carving. After secularization in 1794, the mission fell into disrepair. Church sections which had collapsed in 1868 and in 1928 were restored in 1934–1936 and 1947–1948. San José has functioned as a church since 1937.

The width of San José's west front is 18.6 meters and rises 22.4

FIGURE 7.1. San Antonio (Texas): Mission San José, west front.

FIGURE 7.2. Mission San José, facade.

meters to the top of the belfry cross (Fig. 7.1).[8] The facade, completed by 1785, and possibly as early as 1778, sits between square tower bases, but only the south belfry was finished. Deeply cut flora climb the portal's door jambs (Fig. 7.2), while angels frolic among the garlands twisting around the arch. In the center, they hold Our Lady of Guadalupe aloft. Twisting tendrils in high relief likewise surround the choir window. It is rare for a facade to make an iconographic statement as does this one. Life-size, graceful statues flank the entrance. Mary's father, Saint Joachim, is to the left; her mother, Saint Anne, to the right holding the child, Mary. Saint Joseph (San José), the church's patron, is the topmost statue; Saint Francis is to his left and Saint Dominic to his right.

San José's interior measures 30 by 7.6 meters. Its three rectangular nave bays (7.6 by 5.6) are closed with barrel vaults, 10.6 meters high. The bay next to the apse is square even though there is no transept. Its dome, set upon a pendentive, rises 18 meters from floor level. A two-story convento (40 by 12 meters), now in ruins, is attached to the east wall of the apse. The mission complex, measuring 180 by 143 meters, is surrounded by restored Indian living quarters. Mardith Schuetz considers San José to be the work "of a single master mason, or a team of masons working under the direction of a maestro" and tentatively identifies this person as "master mason, Antonio Salazar."[9]

Mission Nuestra Señora de la Purísima Concepción de Acuña is said to be "the oldest unrestored church structure in the U.S." Architecturally it is the most significant of the five missions in San Antonio. Mission Concepción, first established in 1716 in East Texas, had its San Antonio beginnings on 5 March 1731, when it received the "de Acuña" title to honor the Viceroy. It became the Texas headquarters of the Querétaro college. The permanent stone church was begun about 1740. The convento was completed by 1745; the church was dedicated on 8 December 1755, the feast day of the Immaculate Conception. Secularization, begun in 1794, was completed by 1824. After several decades of various usages the building began to function again as a church in 1855.

The single nave, cruciform church is an imposing mass of limestone with exterior dimensions of 28.8 meters by 14.6 meters.[10] The west front (17.6 by 10 meters) is crowned with twin stone belfries, each 10 meters tall, their sides pierced with arched openings (Fig.

7.3). Set flush with the tower bases, the plain facade was once covered with painted flower work and red and blue quatrefoil patterns. Traces of "frames" etched in the stucco veneer and tiny segments of color can still be seen. Seven windows lighten the massiveness of the west front. Parapets, rising above the nave walls, conceal the vaulting. A restored single-story convento, with a three-arched portería, extends 24 meters from the south tower base.

The top of the facade door is framed with three stone lintels inscribed with a dedication to the Immaculate Conception (Fig. 7.4). In the spandrels are delicate reliefs depicting Franciscan emblems popular at the time: the crossed arms of Christ and Saint Francis on the left, and the five wounds, symbols of the stigmata of Saint Francis, on the right, all masterfully linked by a sinuous Franciscan cord. The

FIGURE 7.3. San Antonio (Texas): Mission Concepción, west front.

FIGURE 7.4. Mission Concepción, facade, portal.

FIGURE 7.5. Mission Concepción, view from rear through crossing into sanctuary.

engaged framing columns are damaged at their base but intact otherwise and covered with floral designs. Deeply incised diamonds pattern the stone wall outside the columns. Crowning the (7 by 4.3) portal is a nearly equilateral stone triangle, its sharp angularity softened by three choir windows.

The 27-meter interior is organized into choir, three nave bays, crossing, and sanctuary, all with a width of 6.6 meters (Fig. 7.5). The rectangular bays, of slightly different sizes, average 3.5 meters in length while the sanctuary is 4 meters deep. Transept arms have the same dimensions as the bays. All bays have barrel vaults 8.6 meters high, as does the sacristy adjoining the south transept arm. The crossing carries a dome, 15 meters high, set on a drum supported by pendentives.

Tower bases house a baptistry and a chapel, both with murals. Restoration completed in 1990 revealed these murals and those in the convento, particularly the one covering a ceiling, to have been executed in a rich panoply of color.

It is extraordinary that on this distant northern Spanish frontier two cruciform churches have their crossings closed with domes set on pendentives. Constructing pendentives requires great architectural skills, a fact which gives backing to Mardith Schuetz's conviction that "professional builders" were present in San Antonio. She speculates that perhaps Estevan de el Oio was "brought north to build the church at Concepción."[11]

The lands surrounding the churches at Concepción, San José, San Juan, and Espada officially became the San Antonio Missions National Park on 1 April 1983. The National Park Service has effected many improvements, including construction of a visitor contact station at Mission Concepción. The larger visitor center at San José opened its doors in 1995. A pamphlet made available by the San Antonio Missions National Historical Park contains a detailed map and graphically tells the story of these four missions and the Coahuiltecan Indians they served.

ΝΕШ ΜΕΧΙϹΟ

In the area around Santa Fe the Spanish encountered peoples whom they named "Pueblo Indians" because they lived in settled communities.[12] By the mid-seventeenth century, twenty-four mission churches had been established by the Franciscans within the pueblo communities around Santa Fe. These churches were destroyed during the Pueblo Revolt of 1680, but almost all were reestablished after the 1692–1694 reconquest.

The pueblo churches of New Mexico are particularly significant because only in that area of all the Southwest did the Spanish missionaries encounter an indigenous building tradition. Nowhere else in Nueva España was the impact of native architecture on Spanish colonial architecture as strong as in the Pueblo world around Santa Fe. While church size and outline were European in origin, mode of construction, texture of walls, and overall statement were distinctly non-European, speaking clearly of a local building tradition. In the Pueblo way of building with adobe and stone, the arch is almost nonexistent and the dome is never seen. The native Indian heritage of construction speaks every bit as forcefully as the imported European shape.

ACOMA

The adobe walls of San Esteban Rey, constructed between 1629 and 1644, rise as sheer as the sides of the mesa where Acoma pueblo has existed for close to 800 years. Majestic in its unbroken mass, the apse (Fig. 7.6) glows warmly in the setting sun.[13] Shadows from exposed ends of cut logs paint the wall in constantly moving murals as the sun arcs through the sky. A small parapet conceals the flat roof, now covered with cement. *Vigas*, logs 36 centimeters in diameter and more than twelve meters in length, span the nave. After vigas were set into the top of the walls, a system of cedar twigs was laid atop the vigas and then covered with a matting of plant fiber and a thick layer of adobe earth. San Esteban's atrio cross and wall with adobe merlons, broad facade, narrow single door, and twin towers echo sixteenth-century Mexico (Fig. 7.7). Yet nowhere else in central Nueva España could one see these soft contours of the atrio wall, the rounded corners of the bell towers, the rippled surface of its earth-covered facade.

FIGURE 7.6. Acoma (New Mexico): Mission San Esteban, west-facing apse.

FIGURE 7.7.
Mission San Esteban,
atrio and east front.

Nave walls, rising 11.4 meters, vary in thickness. The base of the south wall has a width of 1.98 meters, that of the north wall, 2.31 meters.[14] Only two windows, high in the south wall, provide illumination to the interior. The corners of the tower bases and apse are "reinforced" with uncut stone; otherwise San Esteban Rey is entirely adobe. This, the oldest and largest of the extant missions in New Mexico, was not destroyed during the Pueblo Revolt in 1680 although it was likely damaged to some extent. Extensive repairs were made in 1924. For certain, the structure seen today dates from at least 1700. The 39-by-9.4-meter interior is cool, serene, overpowering. There are no bays, no modular rhythms, no pews. The floor is hard-packed earth. The sanctuary is elevated one step; the retablo is lifted three meters above the floor. Never before in the Pueblo world had such an immense, unbroken volume been enclosed.

FIGURE 7.8. Taos (New Mexico): mission church with atrio, from the east.

TAOS AND RANCHO DE TAOS

Taos and Rancho de Taos contain two other intriguing examples of Pueblo-mission architecture. Taos, like Acoma, has been a pueblo for centuries. A traditional way of life continues there, keeping ancient cultural values alive. Electricity, in-door plumbing and many other "modern" conveniences are not wanted.

At Taos, on the edge of a large, open center a thick, soft-walled church and its atrio have been rebuilt to resemble as closely as possible the original, destroyed by fire in 1847. Dwarf bell towers sparkle in the light of the rising sun (Fig. 7.8), since the facade, like Acoma's, faces east. Vibrant earth colors cover the exterior and interior walls of this small, flat-roofed edifice.

The Spanish built their settlement a few miles distant, naming it Rancho de Taos. One of the first structures erected was their parish church, San Francisco, subsequently rebuilt about 1772. Though not a mission church, it is one of the most impressive of the adobe, cruci-form flat-roof structures in the entire Pueblo-mission inventory. Overall dimensions are 36.2 by 10 (nave) by 18.6 (transept) meters.

Few sights are as dramatic and powerful as San Francisco's sun-drenched bulky apse and transept arms (Fig. 7.9).[15] The "bolsters," cushionlike buttresses, are monumental statements of pure form, almost abstract. Though not as stark, the facade also makes a powerful statement with its soft edges and undulant surfaces. Neither apse nor transept are set at an exact right angle to the longitudinal axis of the 8-meter-wide nave. The nave, as well as the 16-meter transept, is spanned by corbelled beams. Set perpendicularly to those of nave and sanctuary, the transept beams cover the crossing.

If it was considered prudent not to puncture the adobe wall of the apse with windows, how then to illuminate the sanctuary? The solution was to build a transverse transom, or clearstory, several feet higher than the nave at the roofline where the transept begins (Fig. 7.10). Since the apse faces west, the clearstory faces east. The rays of the rising sun flood through the clearstory into the sanctuary, dramatically illuminating San Francisco's softly colored wooden retablo and statues.

ARIZONA AND SONORA

Beginning in the middle of the seventeenth century, Jesuit missionaries were active among the Pimas Altas Indians who had long been settled in that area of northern Sonora (Mexico) and southern Arizona

FIGURE 7.9. Rancho de Taos (New Mexico):
San Francisco, west-facing apse, transept.

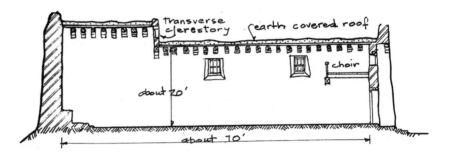

FIGURE 7.10. San Francisco, clearstory at junction of nave and transept.

(up to the Gila River) known as Pimería Alta. The Pima Indians, today known by their ancient name, the O'odham, lived a communal life without, however, establishing any special architectural heritage.[16] In 1687 the Jesuit missionary and cartographer, Eusebio Francisco Kino, arrived in the Pimería Alta. By the time of his death, twenty-four years later in 1711, Father Kino and fellow Jesuits had founded more than two dozen missions. None of the original churches he built still stand; a few remain as archeological ruins. Other Jesuits, and later the Franciscans, subsequently built new churches in many of the original settlements.[17] These eighteenth- and nineteenth-century mission churches are still referred to as "the Kino chain." Three of these are now preserved as part of Tumacácori National Historic Park in southern Arizona, including Mission San José de Tumacácori.

OQUITOA (Sonora)

San Antonio Paduano del Oquitoa is one of the best surviving examples of Jesuit church construction among their missions in the Pimería Alta. As of 1730 a chapel was reported under construction at Oquitoa. "It is almost certainly this building, whose church and sacristy in 1797 provided 'suitable rooms,' whose roof was of beams (as it is today), and which was 'sheathed on the outside with brick and lime mortar,' that is seen today."[18] History has treated San Antonio gently and the church, restored in 1980, probably looks much like it did in the 1730s. Religious services continue to be conducted there.

Atop a knoll, the glistening white church creates a commanding presence despite its small 25-by-6.5-meter exterior (Fig. 7.11) The three-part vertical division of the facade with niches set between shallow pilasters is quite standard; however, a very distinctive molding gently curves to frame the second tier. A countercurve in the third tier leads the eye to the delicate espadaña holding two bells.

The interior is equally simple but eloquent (Fig. 7.12). The clean walls course along unbroken. The long, flat-roofed rectangular nave with no bays features close-set corbelled beams marching stolidly to the triumphal arch. The sanctuary altar is modern.

FIGURE 7.11. Oquitoa (Sonora): Mission San Antonio, west front, facade.

SAN XAVIER DEL BAC (Arizona)

The O'odham community of Bac ("where the water emerges"), still located just to the south of Tucson, was first visited by Father Kino in 1692. He laid the foundations of a mission church, dedicated to his patron San Xavier, in 1700. It was never completed, becoming only little more than a *enramada* (a brush shelter). A proper church was not underway until after the arrival of another Jesuit, Father Alonso Espinosa, in 1756. This second church, flat-roofed and made of adobe, was in use at least by 1763. Beset with many structural problems, it was dismantled in the 1820s for its materials to be used in other mission structures.

As best they could, Franciscan friars replaced the banished Jesuits in the Pimería Alta. Fray Juan Bautista Velderrain arrived in San

FIGURE 7.12. Mission San Antonio,
view from rear to sanctuary.

Xavier del Bac in 1776. Soon thereafter, and under his guidance, the present magnificent complex probably had its beginnings; it was completed under Fray Juan Bautista Llorens in 1797. The architect has been identified as Ignacio Gaona.[19] Documentation shows that the church, as of 1788, had vaulted roofs and was built not of adobe but of fired bricks. Between 1831 and 1873 San Xavier was not staffed by any clergy. The Franciscans returned in 1913 and still minister to the needs of the O'odham Indians.

Mission San Xavier del Bac is a cruciform structure. The interior measures 30 meters on the longitudinal (north-south) axis and 18.5 across the transept (east-west) axis with the crossing being a 6.37-meter square.[20] Widths of nave, sanctuary, and transept bays are a constant 6.58 meters. Lengths, however, vary. The sanctuary (the northernmost bay) is 5 meters deep, transept arms are 6.07, third and second nave bays are 4.85 long with the first, or choir bay, measuring 5.36 meters. Each bay is closed with a shallow brick dome. The crossing has a full dome resting upon a drum with four windows.

Regularly renewed by a coat of lime wash, San Xavier's brilliant white towers and bases provide a most unique "frame" for the warm earth-colored (south) facade (Fig. 7.13). By using fired brick, the builders fashioned a relatively weather-proof facade. Although the composition displays the standard colonial three horizontal tiers and three vertical sections, its execution is distinctive. The estípite columns are unlike any others. The óculo has been transformed into a door leading onto a balcony from which one could easily address those assembled in the atrio. The curves of the crest sway and dip in their own unique fashion. In many ways the facade echoes the main retablo.

The interior of San Xavier del Bac shimmers with color, especially the main retablo (Fig. 7.14). At the top of the fired-brick retablo God the Father, surrounded by angels, smiles benignly upon Mary, directly beneath. The large central figure, just above the altar, is the patron, Francis Xavier, the great Jesuit saint who remained patron even after the Franciscans arrived. The octagon at the crossing is gradually transformed into a dome by concentric rings of brick. From a floral design in the center of the dome a pendant Franciscan cord ties together twenty-four cartouches arranged in three descending tiers of eight cartouches in which coats-of-arms, angels, and Franciscan saints

FIGURE 7.13. Tucson (Arizona): Mission San Xavier del Bac,
south-facing front, facade (Helga Teiwes, Tucson).

are depicted. Each transept arm contains two altars, each with its own
brick retablo as richly colored as the main one. Restoration of the
interior has been underway since 1993 by a world-renowned group.
Restoration of the main retablo, including renewing painted gold-
and silver-leafed surfaces, was achieved during the first quarter of
1995. It was discovered that these surfaces had once been covered
with transparent glazes which gave the retablo a stunning opales-
cence. This beautiful state was hidden for years beneath heavy coats of
varnish that had turned black.[21] Once again a scintillating and colorful
interior delights the beholder. Mission San Xavier del Bac is a
National Historic Landmark.

CALIFORNIA

For some seventy years the Jesuits had been active in Baja California as missionaries prior to their expulsion in 1767. Most vacancies were soon filled by the Franciscans under the leadership of Fray Junípero Serra. He immediately established plans to expand the missions northward into Alta California. Founded on 16 July 1769, Mission San Diego de Alcalá was the first of twenty-one Franciscan missions established by 1823 along the coast of today's California. Nine were founded by Serra.

The natives of Alta California, while depending on hunting, gathering, and fishing for their livelihood, lived in fairly large and fixed villages. Faced with too many native settlements the Franciscans opted for a program of *reducciónes*, enticing or forcing the Indians to live in the mission complexes.

A typical complex consisted of four wings around a central quadrangle.[22] The church usually formed one side of the quadrangle. The front wing, with a long porch attached to it, was generally residential while the other wings contained workshops and warehouses. This long porch, supported by arches, masonry piers, or wooden posts, is a special feature of California mission architecture. Another distinctive feature of some California missions is the free-standing bell tower fashioned as an espadaña, its wall pierced with several openings for various sized bells. San Juan Capistrano typifies the mission complex in California as depicted in the restoration painting (Fig. 7.15). Before its collapse in the December 1812 earthquake, its 44-by-8.5-meter cruciform church would have been the grandest of the California missions. Only the sanctuary remains "intact." Saving it and a few other walls from further deterioration is now the main focus of San Juan's preservation project.

All but three of the California missions had single-nave churches. In plan two were cruciform and the third basilican. Three had masonry vaulted ceilings, all of which failed; others had wooden ceilings, usually flat. Interior walls were generally decorated with murals. Many missions were surprisingly well supplied with imported statuary, paintings on canvas, and prints from Mexico.

During the 1830s and 1840s the new Mexican government decreed the secularization of the California missions. For many the

FIGURE 7.14. Mission San Xavier del Bac, view from rear toward sanctuary (Helga Teiwes, Tucson).

FIGURE 7.15. San Juan Capistrano (California): Mission San Juan Capistrano
before 1812 earthquake, reconstruction painting by Helen Duke
under guidance of Norman Neuerburg (Norman Neuerburg, Los Angeles).

transition to a parish church spelled an architectural disaster. Most
mission churches were abandoned for decades. Adobe walls suffered
severely once the roof gave way. Today most have been reconstructed.
Even in their precarious condition they became the inspiration for the
Mission Revival style, popular in southern California during the
1930s and 1940s.

CARMEL

Mission San Carlos Borromeo de Carmelo was founded on 3 June
1770 by Father Junípero Serra. An adobe church, about 33 by 8
meters, with a thatched roof was finished in 1783. Father Serra, who
died on 27 August 1783, was buried in its sanctuary. The cornerstone
of the present church was laid on 7 July 1793. It is known from
records that the master mason and stonecutter, Manuel Esteban Ruiz,
was involved in constructing this new stone and mortar church. By

FIGURE 7.16. Carmel (California): Mission Carmel, west front, facade
(Norman Neuerburg, Los Angeles).

1795 the tile roof was in place. The new San Carlos Borromeo, dedicated in September 1797, occupied the site of the older adobe structure, leaving Serra's grave undisturbed. The church interior displayed
unique parabolic stone arches and a ceiling of planks. The roof collapsed in 1851 and the interior was in ruins by 1868. A shingle roof
was constructed in 1884 and the church was rededicated in August of
that year. During the 1930s the interior was restored and the roof was
returned to its original form.

Of the original 1795–1797 church two elements remain intact: the
facade and the 8.8-by-46.5-meter plan. Its star-shaped choir window,
seen in no other California mission church, is set slightly askew with

FIGURE 7.17. Santa Barbara (California): Mission Santa Bárbara, west front, neoclassical facade (Norman Neuerburg, Los Angeles).

the points upright instead of diagonally, the normal mode (Fig. 7.16). A hefty belfry and dome anchor the left side, its asymmetry strikingly effective. A fountain was added to the atrio, now filled with flowers. Known today as Mission Carmel, the church still serves the seaside community of Carmel.

SANTA BARBARA

Mission Santa Bárbara Virgen y Mártir was founded 4 December 1786; the quadrangle, completed by 1793, retains its front arched porch. The mission's adobe church was irreparably damaged in the earthquake of December 1812. The present masonry church, begun in 1815, was completed by 10 September 1820. The architect was possibly José Antonio Ramírez. This single-nave church, with a tile gable roof, measures 53 by 11 meters. A second domed belfry was added in 1831, fell in 1832, and was rebuilt in 1833. It is the only twin-tower mission church in California (Fig. 7.17).

The classic facade, constructed between 1815 and 1820, and rebuilt between 1950 and 1952 because of earlier (1925) earthquake damage, was possibly inspired by a book on architecture written by Vitruvius, a first-century Roman. A copy of a 1787 Spanish edition of his book, entitled *Los Diez Libros de Arquitectura*, was found in the mission library. Designed in the manner of a hexastyle Ionic Greek temple, the facade's central intercolumnation is widened to give space for the arched doorway and round choir window. A statue of the patroness stands in a niche in the pediment while statues of Faith, Hope, and Charity adorn the gables.

As noted earlier, neoclassicism was introduced into Nueva España in the 1780s with the establishment of the Royal Academy of San Carlos in Mexico City. It is noteworthy that this "new" style is seen in that most distant Spanish frontier of Alta California as early as the 1790s.[23] Perhaps even more remarkable is that in the early part of the nineteenth century the "domain" of neoclassic architecture extended from Saint Petersburg to Santa Barbara.

N. Scott Momaday, a Native American poet and novelist, speaks to the impact of native cultures on mission architecture of the Southwest: "A special dimension in the story of the missions of the Southwest is the native American intercession. The missions concede something to the Indian world, a simplicity, a touch of the patience and calm, a world view founded upon symmetry and balance, a profound understanding of the earth, water and sky."[24]

SUGGESTED READING

Drain, Thomas A. *A Sense of Mission: Historic Churches of the Southwest*. Photography by David Wakely. Chronicle Books, 1994.

Fontana, Bernard L. *Entrada: The Legacy of Spain and Mexico in the United States*. Southwest Parks and Monuments Association, Tucson, 1994.

Kennedy, Roger G. *Mission: The History and Architecture of the Missions of North America.* Photographs by Michael Freeman. Houghton Mifflin Co., 1993.

Schuetz-Miller, Mardith. "Architecture of the Spanish Borderlands." In *Encyclopedia of the North American Colonies*, vol. III, Charles Scribner's Sons, 1993.

TEXAS

"Cross and Crown: The Spanish Missions in Texas." In *Hispanic Texas: A Historical Guide*, edited by Helen Simons and Cathryn A. Hoyt, pp. 24–35. University of Texas Press, 1992.

Habig, Marion. *The Alamo Chain of Missions.* 2d ed. Franciscan Herald Press, 1976.

NEW MEXICO

Bunting, Bainbridge. *Early Architecture in New Mexico.* University of New Mexico Press, 1976.

Kubler, George. *The Religious Architecture of New Mexico.* University of New Mexico Press, 1990.

Treib, Marc. *Sanctuaries of Spanish New Mexico.* University of California Press, 1993.

ARIZONA

Duell, Prent. *Mission Architecture as Examplified (sic) in San Xavier del Bac.* Arizona Archaeological and Historical Society, Tucson, 1919.

Guide to the Pimería Alta: Missions and More. Southwestern Mission Research Center, Tucson, 1996.

CALIFORNIA

Baer, Kurt. *Architecture of the California Missions.* University of California Press, 1958.

Neuerburg, Norman. "Indian Carved Statues at Mission Santa Barbara." *The Masterkey*, Southwest Museum, Oct.–Dec. 1977, 147–151.

———. "More Indian Sculpture at Mission Santa Barbara." *The Masterkey*, Southwest Museum, Jul.–Sept. 1980, 150–153.

———. "Some Fantasy Views of the California Missions." *The Californians*, Sept.–Oct., 1984, 28–31.

———. *The Decoration of the California Missions*. Bellerophon Books, 1989.

———. "The Alta California Indians as Artists Before and After Contact." (with Georgia Lee), *Columbian Consequences*, vol. I, Smithsonian Institution Press, 1989, 467–480.

———. "Neoclassicism in Spanish California." *La Gazeta del Archivo*, Santa Barbara Mission Archive–Library, Spring 1994, 1–6.

Newcomb, Rexford. *The Franciscan Mission Architecture of Alta California*. Dover Publications, 1973.

Schuetz-Miller, Mardith. *Building and Builders in Hispanic California 1769–1850*. Southwest Mission Research Center, Tucson; Santa Barbara Trust for Historic Preservation, Santa Barbara, 1994.

Notes

━━◆━◇━◆━━

2. Urban Beginnings

1. Dora Crouch, Daniel Garr, and Axel Mundigo, *Spanish City Planning in North America*. A total of 148 ordinances are cited. Planners were able to realize in the New World urban designs impossible to execute in the Old World. Presumably many ordinances were based upon experiences gained in the cities founded earlier in Nueva España.

2. The Tlaxcalans were Cortés's principal allies; they assisted him in capturing the Aztec citadel, Tenochtitlán.

3. Toribio Motolinía, *Motolonía's History of the Indians of New Spain*, 156. Open-air chapels are treated more extensively in Chapter 3.

4. Manuel Toussaint, *Colonial Art in Mexico*, 14.

5. Calle de Macedonia Alcalá 202.

6. Located on Pino Suárez between República and Mesones only a few blocks from the Zócalo.

7. Toussaint, *Colonial Art*, 19.

8. After being abandoned in the nineteenth century the fort served as jail, garrison and naval service center. Today an information center helps reconstruct the fort's history.

9. Mexico City, 1530; Oaxaca, 1535; Pátzcuaro, 1536; Chiapas, 1538; Puebla, 1539; Guadalajara, 1548; Mérida, 1561.

10. Toussaint, *Colonial Art*, 23.

11. The accomplishments of this "newly discovered" architect will be assessed in Chapter 3.

12. Close to the center of the city, the complex of Santo Domingo covers almost a square block. Principal components are church, hospital, residence (*convento*) for the

Dominican friars (now a museum) and, to its north, a residence for novices. The latter is being restored as a cultural center.

3. Sixteenth Century

1. Arthur Ennis, O.S.A., "The Conflict between the Regular and Secular Clergy," in Richard Greenleaf (ed.), *The Roman Catholic Church in Colonial Latin America*, 65.

2. Robert J. Mullen, *The Architecture and Sculpture of Oaxaca: 1530s–1980s*, Ch. 2.

3. During the 1992 visit of Pope John Paul II to Mexico, the open-air church in Cuilapan was once again needed to accommodate the multitudes.

4. One of the largest atrios in Mexico is that of the former Franciscan complex in Izamal, Yucatán.

5. Counterclockwise movement was a prominent feature of ancient ceremonies.

6. John McAndrew, *The Open-Air Churches of Sixteenth-Century Mexico*, 32.

7. Cuernavaca had long been the favorite summering place for the Aztec rulers.

8. Joining an open-air chapel at a right angle to a church facade does not appear again.

9. Toussaint, *Colonial Art*, 55.

10. This is consistent with the Mesoamerican custom of inscriptions reflecting completion, not beginnings. The style and execution of the eagle's feathers, headdress, and speech scrolls in the date stone are other typical prehispanic forms.

11. Toussaint, *Colonial Art*, 50.

12. The nave walls of the Augustinian church in Ixmiquilpan (Hidalgo) are decorated with frescoes of mythological and war scenes, painted in vivid colors by Indian artists. Pieces of black "cloth" are secured by this same knot.

13. Factual data on Dominican sites were derived from the official records, or Actas, of the chapter meetings held regularly by the Dominicans between the years 1540 and 1590. Friars were "assigned" to pueblos; conventos were "accepted" in perpetuity. The history of the Dominican Order in Mexico for this period is described in Chapter 3 of Robert J. Mullen, *Dominican Architecture in Sixteenth-Century Oaxaca*.

14. In a document dated 9 July 1692, the Dominicans and civil authorities, noting that San Pedro y San Pablo was so small it could not contain the numbers attending Mass, agreed to enlarge the church by making a transept (and apse), and "on that very day" started to lay the foundations in trenches already prepared. Document cited in Mullen, *Architecture and Sculpture*, 166.

15. McAndrew, *Open-Air Churches*, 547.

16. George Kubler, *Mexican Architecture of the Sixteenth Century*, 402–416. Kubler dates this facade "in the last quarter of the century" (p. 271).

17. Luis Brozon MacDonald, "La primitiva portada de la iglesia del convento de Santo Domingo de Yanhuitlán, Oax.," *Boletín No. 1—Monumentos Históricos*, Instituto Nacional de Antropología e Historia, Mexico City, 1978.

18. Mullen, *Dominican Architecture*, 139.

19. Francisco de Burgoa, *Geográfica descripción*, I, 291–295.

20. Agustín Dávila Padilla, *Historia . . . de la Orden de Predicadores*, 238–244. "Trazábales las iglesias y casas de comunidad como arquitecto, y servíales en ellas de mayordomo cuando le daban lugar las ocupaciones. . . ."

21. Fray Marín was the architect for two more churches. An assessment of his accomplishments appears at the end of this chapter.

22. The influence of Rodrigo Gil de Hontañón on Dominican architecture both in Spain and Nueva España is traced in Mullen, *Dominican Architecture*, Chapter 7. See also Sergio Luis Sanabria, "The Mechanization of Design in the 16th Century: The Structural Formulae of Rodrigo Gil de Hontañón," *Journal of the Society of Architectural Historians* (December 1982), 285, 286.

23. The height of the two towers nearest the church has been so reduced they are not easily recognizable.

24. Perhaps the nine entrances in each wall (a tenth enters the sanctuary) and the thirteen arches in each arcade express Mesoamerican beliefs that "nine" and "thirteen" designated something highly sacred.

25. Does having nine arches reflect ancient symbolism?

26. Toussaint summarizes the cathedral architects on pages 109–115 of his *Colonial Art in Mexico*.

27. Toussaint, *Colonial Art*, 82–109.

28. Fray Francisco Marín's nine assignments were: 1541—Teposcolula; 1546—Coixtlahuaca; 1547—Oaxaca; 1548—Teposcolula; 1550—Yanhuitlán; 1552—Izúcar; 1553—Teposcolula; 1555—Tonalá; 1556—Chilac; 1559—deceased.

29. Toussaint, *Colonial Art*, attributes Yanhuitlán and Coixtlahuaca "to the same architect . . . ." (p. 106).

30. Kubler, *Mexican Architecture*, v. 1, 242.

31. Spiro Kostov, *A History of Architecture*, 513.

4. Cathedrals

1. A cathedral plan looks like a nave with four aisles. The "third and fourth" aisles are enclosed bays, not interconnected, used as chapels.

2. The hall church, with its derivation in the medieval German *Hallenkirche*, became popular in Spain by the fifteenth century.

3. As illustrated by Víctor Manuel Villegas in "Epílogo," *Catedrales de México*, 258–261. Similar drawings are made of the cathedrals in México, Guadalajara, Puebla.

4. When the Diocese of México was approved in December 1527, construction of the first cathedral began. This structure was demolished in 1626. A royal decree was issued as early as 1536 ordering the construction of a new cathedral.

5. Its history is complex and is still being debated.

6. A fire in 1967 damaged this screen, many of the late-seventeenth-century choir stalls behind it, and the (1692) organ. All have been restored.

7. The original proportions were retained. The height of the towers (without crosses) fits a square determined by the base of the west front. The neoclassic church to its right is the Sagrario, a parish church.

8. These too replaced an older structure.

9. Very tall towers are characteristic of many churches in the State of Puebla, as are tile-covered domes.

10. A full account of these three building stages is found in Robert Mullen, *The Architecture and Sculpture of Oaxaca, 1530s–1980s.*

11. Heinrich Berlin, "Arquitectura y arquitectos coloniales de Oaxaca: La Catedral," *Archivo Español de Arte* (Madrid: 1979), Volume LII, No. 207, 308.

12. Raising the roof height 1.25 meters during the 1660s apparently was not a satisfactory solution.

13. As a result of a devastating earthquake in 1714 the Cathedral was closed until 1733. By 1750 the towers had been reconstructed. The facade, which only needed repairs, had a new crest added. After 1752 no structural change was made to the Cathedral until 1890 when a belfry and clock replaced the crest. During 1978 major restoration work was undertaken.

14. Others are San Luis Potosí, Chihuahua, Fresnillo, Pinos.

15. Nave bays are 10 by 13.5 meters; aisles 10 by 10. The crossing is 13.5 by 13.5.

16. It was the capital of both Coahuila and Texas from 1835 to 1847. Washington-on-the-Brazos was the first capital of the Republic of Texas; the capital was later moved to Austin.

17. A Latin inscription above the center niche reads: "Church of St. James Apostle Major. About 1745—1800. Construction: 93,000 pesos."

5. Transitional Phase

1. Toussaint, *Colonial Architecture*, 180.

2. *Ibid.*, 190.

3. Elizabeth Wilder Weismann, *Art and Time in Mexico*, 47, 49.

4. Octavio Paz, "Will for Form," *Mexico: Splendors of Thirty Centuries*, 24, 25.

5. This event before the Bishop is recorded as having taken place on the ninth or twelfth of December, 1531. Like the Shroud of Turin the image has been analyzed scientifically. It is not "painted" with pigments. The *tilma*, measuring about seventy inches in length and some thirty in width, is described as made of *iczotl*, a wild palm. When woven into material iczotl normally disintegrates after about thirty years, but the *tilma* has remained intact and the image fresh after more than 450 years.

6. Toussaint, *Colonial Art*, 196. The church is located at the intersection of Madero and Isabel la Católica, in the area of the Palacio de Bellas Artes.

7. Located at Vizcaínas and Eje Central Lázaro Cárdenas. "The plans seem to have been drawn by Don Pedro Bueno Basorí . . . and . . . the master architect Miguel José de Quiera who perhaps built it." (Toussaint, *Colonial Art*, 309.)

8. San Sebastián, a much smaller church, once occupied the same location. It had become a very popular pilgrimage site because of its famous statue. When the original church became too small to accommodate the crowds, a new church was erected and named La Soledad. The interior was refurbished in the nineteenth century.

9. Though much has been written about La Soledad, the architect remains anonymous.

10. Toussaint, *Colonial Art*, 195.

11. *Ibid.*, 203.

12. During the Viceregency devotion to the rosary grew quite strong, and a number of chapels were built dedicated to Our Lady of the Rosary.

13. The historian Gay says that a maestro from Puebla was called upon in 1659 to do the stucco and gilt work of the nave vault for which he was paid the large sum of 26,691 pesos. (José Gay, *Historia de Oaxaca*, 3rd ed., v. 1, part 2, 307.)

14. The rich mines of this region have been exploited since antiquity. New processing methods expanded the industry during colonial times.

15. A number of monographs exist, but there are only two known regional studies of Mexico's colonial architecture: Mullen, *The Architecture and Sculpture of Oaxaca, 1530s–1980s*, and Clara Bargellini, *La arquitectura de la plata*.

16. During the seventeenth century ceramics took on extraordinary importance. The Puebla-ware called *talavera* was developed to a high level; it was the only product that could compete with Chinese porcelain. It then took on an architectural role and whole facades of buildings were covered with glazed tiles, called *azulejos*. There are many such in Puebla with patterns reminiscent of Moorish tilework. A fine example in Mexico City is the House of the Conde del Valle de Orizaba (Madero 4), known as the "Casa de los Azulejos" or "House of Tiles."

17. Toussaint, *Colonial Art*, 206.

18. A paved road, branching south from Highway 160 between Cuautla and Izúcar de Matamoros, provides easy access.

19. Their function remains unknown.

6. The Age of Fulfillment, 1750–1800

1. Weismann, *Art and Time in Mexico*, 49. It is ironic that the term *Churrigueresque* has almost nothing to do with the art of the Churriguera brothers in Spain.

2. Johanna Hecht, in *Mexico, Splendors of Thirty Centuries*, 357.

3. A cathedral is a diocesan church. Often attached to it is a parish church, known as the Sagrario.

4. Weismann, *Art and Time in Mexico*, 61.

5. José de la Borda, born in 1699, emigrated to Nueva España as a young man. By 1744 he owned several silver mines near Taxco. One particular vein produced extraordinary amounts—and, of course, profits. Soon a very wealthy man, Borda made his famous pledge. Bustling silversmith workshops and picturesque scenery attract many tourists to Taxco, now a large pueblo.

6. Elisa Vargas Lugo, *La Iglesia de Santa Prisca de Taxco, México*. This splendid book provides documentary details, complete descriptions and exhaustive analysis.

7. Weismann, *Art and Time in Mexico*, 61.

8. *Ibid.*, 170.

9. Toussaint, *Colonial Art*, 282.

10. The relief depicts that moment after Christ's resurrection when the Master bids Thomas to end his doubts by placing his hand in the spear wound. Next to Christ's head the dated inscription can be found.

11. The full name is Antigua Casa de los Condes de San Mateo Valparaíso. It is located at the intersection of Isabel la Católica and Carranza, just two blocks from the Cathedral.

12. Located in the middle of the block on Madero between Bolivar and Gante, a few blocks from the Cathedral.

13. Toussaint, *Colonial Art*, 329.

14. Weismann, *Art and Time in Mexico*, 253. A number of hacienda buildings are illustrated (pp. 255–268), chapels being among the most attractive.

7. Frontier Mission Architecture

1. The capital of today's New Mexico, Santa Fe is the oldest capital city in the United States. Recent research shows Santa Fe may have had its beginnings as early as 1606.

2. Ecclesiastically, a mission is considered a temporary category on the way to becoming a parish.

3. Mardith Schuetz, "Professional Artisans in the Hispanic Southwest. The Churches of San Antonio, Texas," *The Americas*, Academy of American Franciscan History, Vol. XL, July 1983, 18, 19.

4. The military garrison assigned to a presidio offered protection to a mission. Normally a presidio had its own chapel.

5. Schuetz, "Professional Artisans," 20.

6. *Ibid.* 21.

7. *Ibid.*, 33.

8. Measurements were derived from Historic American Buildings Survey (HABS) drawings.

9. Schuetz, "Professional Artisans", 30, 31.

10. Measurements were derived from HABS drawings.

11. Schuetz, "Professional Artisans," 26.

12. As early as A.D. 1000 the peoples living in the "Four Corners" region of Utah, Colorado, Arizona, and New Mexico had developed a communal life organized around kivas and closely linked structures of stone and adobe.

13. Its location perhaps dictated the reverse of the usual orientation: the facade faces east.

14. Measurements for the churches of New Mexico were taken from George Kubler's *Religious Architecture of New Mexico*.

15. Often the subject of artists, San Francisco is perhaps the most photographed or painted architectural structure of the Southwest.

16. The Tohono O'odham ("Desert People") are the Papago; the Akimel O'odham ("River People") are the Pimas.

17. In 1767, believing the Society of Jesus constituted a threat to his sovereignty, Charles III banished the Jesuits, more than 5,000 of them, from throughout the Spanish empire and recalled them to Spain. Many who had labored in the Southwest had come from central Europe.

18. *Guide to the Pimería Alta: Missions and More*, 96. Dedicated to Saint Anthony of Padua, the church never achieved the rank of parish; it was initially subject to nearby Caborca.

19. Mardith Schuetz-Miller, personal communication, 1996.

20. Dr. Bernard L. Fontana, in a personal communication, supplied exact measurements as derived from HABS drawings.

21. Fontana, involved for years in the preservation and restoration of San Xavier del Bac, supplied the most recent details of the restored murals in a personal communication. San Xavier has been described as the "Sistine Chapel of the United States."

22. Dr. Norman Neuerburg, in a personal communication, kindly provided extensive detailed information on the California missions, including manuscript essays, articles and books. His "Neoclassicism in Spanish California" was a revelation. He is also coauthor of *California Missions to Cut Out, Books I and II*, (Santa Barbara: Bellerophon Books, 1993). Although designed for schoolchildren, the text in no way speaks down to them. Dr. Neuerburg is a renowned scholar of the California missions and has been active in the restoration of a number of those missions.

23. Neuerburg details the rather widespread usage of neoclassic motifs in Alta California in his *The Decoration of the California Missions*.

24. Excerpt from N. Scott Momaday's "Foreword," in Thomas A. Drain's *A Sense of Mission: Historic Churches of the Southwest*.

Glossary

actas: Official account of the meetings, known as Chapters, held periodically by designated friars from the Dominican Province of Santiago, Mexico.

adobe: Sun-dried mud brick.

alfarje: Wooden ceiling of many short pieces, ingeniously fitted together to form a three-sided enclosure with interlaced patterns. Moorish origin.

alfiz: Rectangular or square framing device marking the ornamented part of a portal. Moorish origin.

apse: Terminal part of a church enclosing the sanctuary with its altar; usually the east end.

artesonado: Wooden ceiling with many deep coffers decorated with painting and inlay. Moorish origin.

ashlar: Hewn or squared stone cut to fit a certain location.

atrio: Large walled area usually in front of the church, often seen with atrio cross and corner posas.

azulejos: Glazed tiles, colored, used to cover building surfaces.

barrel vault: Semicircular masonry vault covering a nave.

basilica: Three-aisled structure whose center aisle, the nave in a church, is higher than the side aisles; windows provide illumination to the center.

bay: Defined portion of the nave (or apse).

camarín: Special room for displaying and dressing a sacred image, usually of the Virgin Mary.

capilla de indios: An open-air chapel designed for use by the indigenous (Indian) population.

capilla mayor: Area around the main altar, usually the sanctuary, but can extend into the crossing and transept.

cargo: Pueblo, part of a parish, for which the pastor is held responsible; a dependency of a parish.

Classic Order: An architectural "order" consisting of column, capital, entablature and pediment of Greek Doric, Ionic, and Corinthian temples.

cloister court: Court, forming the core of a convento, bounded by covered walks.

codex/codices: Prehispanic, and at times colonial, manuscripts.

colegio: A school devoted to teaching European culture to different age groups of both sexes.

convent: Religious institution for women; usually cloistered.

convento: Single or two-story residence for friars assigned to a given pueblo, usually placed to the south of the church; often synonymous with the entire complex.

coro: screened area at rear of a convent church reserved for nuns.

crossing: Where the two axes of a church intersect; in plan a square.

doctrina: Pueblos in which the doctrines of the church were taught under the jurisdiction of a parish.

ensamblador: A joiner or carpenter who assembles a retablo.

entablature: Group of horizontal members resting on columns or pilasters of one of the Classic Orders.

espadaña: Wall flush with, but above, the facade pierced with arched openings containing bells; used instead of a tower.

estípite: A "column" square in plan with tapered bottom and formed of several sections giving the appearance of stacked parts.

mampostería: Stone rubble and cement mixed to form a wall; at times covered with a coat of stucco.

merlon: Short decorative element, square with a pyramidal peak, often seen on atrio walls.

mission: Temporary category of a church on its way to becoming a parish.

mudéjar: Culture of the Moors in Spain, or under Spanish rule; a Moorish design.

nave: Longitudinal axis of a single-nave church extending either to transept or to sanctuary; the great central space in a basilica.

óculo: Window, usually circular, placed in a church facade above the main entrance to provide light to the choir.

palacio: Fashionable city residence, usually of wealthy landowners.

parapet: Wall projecting above the roof line to conceal the vaulting.

parroquia: Parish church with resident pastor.

pediment: In Greek architecture the triangular, topmost feature of the Classic Order; in Renaissance and neoclassic architecture a triangular decorative feature, often part of a facade.

pilaster: Flat, vertical member projecting from the wall with column-like features derived from one of the Classic Orders; a decorative element.

portería: Arcaded open porch or vestibule at the main entrance to a convento where visitors were received or could wait for the appearance of a friar.

posa: One of four small chapels in the corners of an atrio at which a pause was made during religious processions around the atrio; often had an altar.

reja: Large metal screen extending from floor to ceiling in a convent church which separates the nuns in their coro from the public attending Mass.

retablo: Gilt altarpiece consisting of many sections of paintings or sculptures. English: "retable."

retablo mayor: The retablo occupying the entire (east) end of the sanctuary/apse wall.

sanctuary: Area, enclosed by the apse, containing the altar; often referred to as chancel.

spandrel: Space between exterior curve of an arch and an enclosing right angle.

talud and tablero: A distinctive prehispanic building form consisting of a large rectangular panel (*tablero*) set upon a smaller outward sloping base (*talud*).

tequitqui: Relief sculpture, usually associated with sixteenth-century Mexico, combining European motifs with an indigenous sense of pattern and technique resulting in a flat surface with sharply profiled designs.

tezontle: Volcanic stone used by builders especially in the city of Mexico; colors range from deep red to rosy tan.

transept: Cross arms, set at ninety degrees to the longitudinal axis, to form a cruciform church.

triumphal arch: Largest arch in a church; proclaims entrance into the sanctuary.

vault: Ceiling or roof of brick or stone built on the principle of the arch.

very large: Church whose length is 55 meters (180') or more.

viga: A log laid across the top of a wall, often extending beyond it, to form a roof structure.

visita: Pueblo with a church but without a resident pastor; a dependency of a parish periodically visited by the pastor or assistant.

zócalo: A name with nineteenth-century origins sometimes given to a city's main plaza, as, for example, that in Mexico City.

Bibliography

Baer, Kurt. *Architecture of the California Missions*. Berkeley: University of California Press, 1958.

Baird, Joseph A. *The Churches of Mexico, 1530–1810*. Berkeley: University of California Press, 1962.

Bargellini, Clara. *La arquitectura de la plata: Iglesias monumentales del centro-norte de México*. Mexico City: UNAM, Instituto de Investigaciones Estéticas, 1991.

Bunting, Bainbridge. *Early Architecture in New Mexico*. Albuquerque: University of New Mexico Press, 1976.

Burgoa, Francisco de. *Geográfica descripción*. Mexico City, 1934.

Catedrales de México. Mexico City, 1993.

———. *Palestra historial de virtudes y exemplares apostólicos*. Mexico City, 1934.

Cook, Sherburne F., and W. W. Borah. *The Indian Population of Central Mexico, 1531–1610*. Berkeley: University of California Press, 1960.

Crouch, Dora, Daniel Garr, and Axel Mundigo. *Spanish City Planning in North America*. Cambridge, Mass.: MIT Press, 1982.

Dávila Padilla, Agustín. *Historia . . . de la Orden de Predicadores*. Mexico City: Editorial Academia Literaria, 1955.

Drain, Thomas A. *A Sense of Mission: Historic Churches of the Southwest*. Photography by David Wakely. San Francisco: Chronicle Books, 1994.

Fontana, Bernard L. *Entrada: The Legacy of Spain and Mexico in the United States*. Tucson: Southwest Parks and Monuments Association, 1994.

Gay, José. *Historia de Oaxaca*, 3d ed., 2 vols. Prólogo de Jorge Fernando Iturribarría. Mexico City, 1950.

Gibson, Charles. *The Aztecs under Spanish Rule: A History of the Valley of Mexico, 1519–1810.* Stanford: Stanford University Press, 1964.

———. *Tlaxcala in the Sixteenth Century.* New Haven: Yale University Press, 1949.

Greenleaf, Richard (ed.). *The Roman Catholic Church in Colonial Latin America.* Tempe: Arizona State University, Center for Latin American Studies, 1977.

Guide to the Pimería Alta: Missions and More. Tucson: Southwestern Mission Research Center, 1996.

Habig, Marion. *The Alamo Chain of Missions*, 2d ed. Chicago: Franciscan Herald Press, 1976.

Kelemen, Pál. *Baroque and Rococo in Latin America.* New York: Thomas Y. Crowell, 1969.

Kennedy, Roger G. *Mission: The History and Architecture of the Missions of North America.* Photographs by Michael Freeman. Boston: Houghton Mifflin Co., 1993.

Kostov, Spiro. *A History of Architecture.* Oxford: Oxford University Press, 1985.

Kubler, George. *Mexican Architecture of the Sixteenth Century.* Westport, Conn.: Greenwood Press, 1972. Originally published in 1948 by Yale University Press, New Haven. 2 vols.

———. *The Religious Architecture of New Mexico.* Albuquerque: University of New Mexico Press, 1990 (5th printing).

McAndrew, John. *The Open-Air Churches of Sixteenth-Century Mexico: Atrios, Posas, Open Chapels, and Other Studies.* Cambridge, Mass.: Harvard University Press, 1965.

Mexico: Splendors of Thirty Centuries. Introduction by Octavio Paz. New York: Metropolitan Museum of Art, A Bullfinch Press Book, 1990.

Motolinía, Toribio. *Motolonía's History of the Indians of New Spain.* Washington, D.C.: Academy of American Franciscan History, 1951.

Mullen, Robert. *The Architecture and Sculpture of Oaxaca, 1530s–1980s.* Tempe: Arizona State University, Center for Latin American Studies, 1995.

———. *Dominican Architecture in Sixteenth-Century Oaxaca.* Tempe: Arizona State University, Center for Latin American Studies, 1975.

Neuerburg, Norman. *The Decoration of the California Missions.* Santa Barbara: Bellerophon Books, 1989.

———. "Neoclassicism in Spanish California." *La Gazeta del Archivo,* Santa Barbara Mission Archive–Library, Spring 1944.

———. "Some Fantasy Views of the California Missions." *The Californians,* September–October 1984.

Newcomb, Rexford. *The Franciscan Mission Architecture of Alta California.* New York: Dover Publications, 1973.

Schuetz-Miller, Mardith. "Architecture of the Spanish Borderlands." In *Encyclopedia of the North American Colonies,* vol. III. New York: Charles Scribner's Sons, 1993.

———. *Building and Builders in Hispanic California 1769–1850.* Tucson: Southwest Mission Research Center, and Santa Barbara: Santa Barbara Trust for Historic Preservation, 1994.

Toussaint, Manuel. *La Catedral de México, México.* Mexico City: Editorial Porrua, 1973.

———. *Colonial Art in Mexico.* Translated and edited by Elizabeth Wilder Weismann. Austin: University of Texas Press, 1967.

Treib, Marc. *Sanctuaries of Spanish New Mexico.* Berkeley: University of California Press, 1993.

Vargas Lugo, Elisa. *La Iglesia de Santa Prisca de Taxco, México.* Mexico City: UNAM, Instituto de Investigaciones Estéticas, 1974.

Weismann, Elizabeth Wilder. *Art and Time in Mexico.* New York: Harper & Row, 1985; Icon paperback, 1995.

———. *Mexico in Sculpture, 1521–1821.* Cambridge, Mass.: Harvard University Press, 1950.

Index

✦

Page numbers in italics refer to illustrations.